CLIMB GLACIER
NATIONAL PARK

ILLUSTRATED ROUTES FOR BEGINNING AND INTERMEDIATE CLIMBERS

VOLUME TWO: THE TWO MEDICINE VALLEY AND FIREBRAND PASS

Scott.

Climbing Routes in Photos

Even more to explore.

See the Route ... *Stand on top!*
Follow the Route.

Have fun climbing
John VanHuudoule

Christmas 2012

Climb Glacier National Park
Illustrated Routes for Beginning and Intermediate Climbers

Volume Two: The Two Medicine Valley And Firebrand Pass

Blake Passmore
with John VanArendonk, Scott Burry and Brad Roy

© 2012 Blake Passmore

ISBN: 1-931291-94-2

Library of Congress Control Number: 2011921278
First Edition

Published and Printed In The United States Of America

All Rights Reserved

Unattributed photographs are by Blake Passmore.

Published and Distributed by:
Montana Outdoor Guidebooks, LLC
175 Hutton Ranch Rd., Ste. 103 PMB 333
Kalispell, MT 59901
www.climbglacier.com
E-mail: climbglacier@gmail.com

For more information visit: **www.climbglacier.com**

Also available from:
Stoneydale Press Publishing Company
523 Main Street   PO Box 188
Stevensville, Montana 59870
Phone: 406-777-2729
E-mail: stoneydale@montana.com

Do you come here often?

Oh sure... As often as possible. Because when I'm face to face with these peaks there are no greater mountains on the planet. I mean, I know that's not true, but during the time spent on them... in their midst... no other possibility exists. To use a kind of common vernacular that gives a sense of perspective... well, they'll just about blow the top of your head off.

Yeah, I keep coming back. It feels good as the everyday layers peel away, feels good to fill my mind with what is here. But I do admit that it gets harder to leave all the time. This place has a certain quality about it – I guess maybe you'd call it wildness – which in no way can be avoided, or ignored... not that that's the sort of thing you'd ever consider resisting. And even though that quality isn't in the least compatible with life back home, invariably causing no end of conflict and depression through drawn-out days of ordinariness, and despite that you know perfectly well those feelings will happen every time... still – you can't help but take them with you. Sometimes it is really tough leaving. You keep looking over your shoulder.

So anyway... yes. I come here whenever possible. Always will.

Written by Vernon Garner

This book is dedicated to the memory of Vernon Garner, known as "Saintgrizzly" to SummitPost.org readers.

Vernon lost a courageous battle with cancer on March 1, 2011. "Saintgrizzly" loved to explore the high country. His writings inspired many readers to get out and explore Glacier National Park. His passion for life and enthusiasm for climbing was infectious. He is greatly missed!

Excerpts of Vernon's writing are found in the Overview sections for Rising Wolf Mountain, Grizzly Mountain, Sinopah Mountain, and Flinsch Peak in this Volume of

Climb Glacier National Park.

Photos and selected writings are used with permission from Vernon's family.

Vernon Garner
1946 - 2011

Vernon Garner on the summit of Gunsight Mountain, Glacier National Park.

Table of Contents

Featured Peaks

Bonus Peaks

Appendix

Legal Notice:

"Climb Glacier National Park" is NOT a training manual for climbing in Glacier National Park. Climbing is a dangerous sport. The author and publisher of this book are not responsible if you or your party are injured while climbing.

You assume risk any time you climb. Before starting this great adventure of climbing educate yourself about the proper equipment, techniques, and safety practices that will help you to be a competent mountaineer. Purchase and carry the equipment that is needed to climb safely to the summits. Climb with groups that have experienced leaders and wear your climbing helmet!

There are inherent risks, dangers, hazards, and such in mountaineering, climbing and rappelling activities. Participation in such activities and/or use of such equipment may result in injury or illness including, but not limited to bodily injury, disease, strains, fractures, partial and/or total paralysis, death or other ailments that could cause serious disability.

These risks and dangers may be caused by negligence of the participants, the negligence of others, accidents, the forces of nature, or other causes. Risks and dangers may arise from foreseeable or unforeseeable causes including, but not limited to poor decision-making, including misjudging terrain, trail, falling, and other such risks, hazards and dangers that are integral to recreational activities and/or use of equipment.

In Other Words ... Don't Do Stupid Stuff!

Featured Peaks are **Named** and shown with ○.

Bonus Peaks are **Named** and shown with ●.

Trailheads are marked with this **color**.

Please refer to each peak section for trailhead, on-trail route, climbing routes as well as all the other juicy details related to each mountain, mount, or peak.

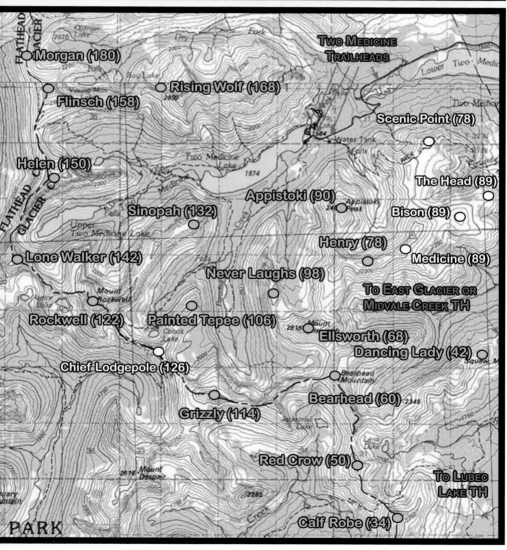

Morgan (180)

Rising Wolf (168)

Two Medicine Trailheads

Flinsch (158)

Scenic Point (78)

Helen (150)

The Head (89)

Appistoki (90)

Sinopah (132)

Bison (89)

Henry (78)

Lone Walker (142)

Medicine (89)

Never Laughs (98)

To East Glacier or Midvale Creek TH

Rockwell (122)

Painted Tepee (106)

Ellsworth (68)

Dancing Lady (42)

Chief Lodgepole (126)

Bearhead (60)

Grizzly (114)

Red Crow (50)

To Lubec Lake TH

PARK

Calf Robe (34)

ACKNOWLEDGMENTS:

VOLUME TWO: THE TWO MEDICINE VALLEY AND FIREBRAND PASS is written for begin
ning and intermediate climbers who want to explore Glacier National Park's high coun
try. This volume contains **suggested** routes to the summits of 22 peaks. There obviousl
are more than one way to reach the summits of most peaks. This area is a great place t
GET OUT AND EXPLORE!

Those who already climb in Glacier would question why another book is needed and stat
that with all of the illustrated photos, maps, and GPS and UTM coordinates the challeng
of climbing is gone. This book is not for climbers who are already proficient at route find
ing and want to climb without additional help. If this book saves one life and if anothe
falls in love with the peaks in Glacier National Park, this work will have met its goal c
inspiring others to explore. So use the book for its intended purpose; use the illustration
maps, and coordinates to safely navigate amongst Glacier's peak.

Few of us would be climbing in the park without A Climber's Guide To Glacier Nationa
Park by J. Gordon Edwards. His book has been the "bible" for climbing in the park fo
years and failure to recognize this work would be unthinkable. A few of his routes ar
featured in this book, but they are updated using current technology such as color pho
tographs with suggested routes, trail and route waypoints, and color maps meant to mak
the routes easier to follow.

Above all, eternal thanks to God, my heavenly Father, the Creator of this awesome place
You have been here from the beginning and when I stand on the summits I see you
handiwork displayed!

Thank you to my incredible wife, Kathleen, for understanding, supporting, and endurin
this obsession of climbing. Thank you for believing in me, sharing your life with me, an
giving me the space to pursue dreams. You make everyday of my life better and you wil
always have my heart! You give me a reason to come home every day.

To my children, Brendan and his wife Julie, Alyssa, and Bhavani; you are my inspiratio
to live life to its fullest and always climb safe in the high country.

To my friends and contributing authors, John VanArendonk, Scott Burry and Brad Roy
you guys rock! Thanks for your support and encouragement.

To all of the crew who climbed with me while working on the routes for Volume Two
Thanks for helping me with this project! These guys and gals answered the call and w
had a great time exploring Glacier National Park.

The 2011 CLIMB GLACIER NATIONAL PARK Team was: Tim Bachman, Fran
(aka *The Ironman*) Barthel, Kim Bergi, Scott Burry, Matt Fitzwater, Joey Gardner, Kri
Gross, Mike Gross, Rod Graham, Austin Hughes, Becky Neumann, Isaiah Neumann
Matt Reiger, Chris Rost, Kristy Rost, Bob Sihler, Mike Thompson, Micah Tinkham, Joh
VanArendonk, Mike VanArendonk, and Read Vaughan.

Trisha Burry ... thank you for all of your work on the cover! Kris Gross ... thanks for de
signing the logo for the book series. I hope you go far in your career.

NOTE TO THE READER:

Thank you for purchasing "CLIMB GLACIER NATIONAL PARK." Consider this guidebook your passport to new experiences in Glacier National Park!

There are 234 named peaks or points, 734 miles (1181 km) of trails, 762 lakes, and 26 glaciers in Glacier National Park. Most visitors take it all in by driving over Going-to-the-Sun Highway and see just a few of her mountains, dip their toes in just a handful of the lakes, view Jackson Glacier, a few even hike on the remote trails. Of those who venture on to the trails an even smaller percentage experience Glacier "off-trail."

You must have different dreams and goals for your time spent here. You want a more intimate experience. You want to be inspired! You want to stand on the summits and see the vistas … you are a climber.

The twenty-two peaks featured in this volume are located in the southwestern corner of Glacier National Park. The Two Medicine and Firebrand Pass areas are more isolated and therefore climbers can easily find solitude. Beginning or intermediate climbers can explore them and enjoy incredible views from each summit.

The routes featured in this book are not advanced routes. Advanced routes for selected peaks throughout Glacier National Park may be featured in future volumes of "CLIMB GLACIER NATIONAL PARK.

The views from the summits featured in this guidebook are phenomenal to say the least. Plan to see other visitors as mere specks down on the roads and trails in the lush green valleys.

Climbing Glacier National Park's peaks and sharing them with others has long been a passion of the writers. We trust that you, too, will thoroughly enjoy each moment you spend amongst the summits of Glacier National Park! Be safe on those summits!

Visit On-line @
WWW.CLIMBGLACIER.COM

Blake Passmore was born in the Flathead valley where he works as a mental health professional. He and his wife, Kathleen, feel blessed to be able to raise their children, Brendan, Alyssa, and Bhavani in the valley. They have incredible friends and a supportive extended family. In addition to spending time with friends and family in Glacier, Blake enjoys fly-fishing, running, mountain biking, and photography.

Blake discovered a passion for writing about his climbing experiences in Glacier National Park. As a frequent contributor for an on-line climbing community he has written on 30 peaks, 29 routes, and over 20 articles to help others enjoy the place he loves so much. He is hoping to help others enjoy the experience of standing on the summits of Glacier National Park. He has discovered that there are always more peaks to climb!

Blake has been to many summits in Glacier. He has climbed many of them multiple times. Some of his favorite summit views are from Mount Cleveland, Never Laughs Mountain, Chief Mountain, Rising Wolf Mountain, Heavens Peak, and Lone Walker Mountain. Next year there may a different list of favorites. Glacier National Park is full of potential favorite summits for everyone! He is a member of the Glacier Mountaineering Society.

In photo: Scott Burry, John VanArendonk, and Blake Passmore

Photo by Ben VanArendonk.

One challenge while climbing in the park was locating the correct route and completing climbs. Many of the route descriptions are difficult to follow due to changes in climate, topography and even trail locations. This guidebook is a solution to the problem and he plans to add additional guidebooks to cover other popular areas of Glacier National Park.

John VanArendonk was born in Montana but raised and educated in Michigan. He moved back to Montana 24 years ago largely because of his love of climbing mountains. Ever since beginning to climb in Junior High at various Rocky Mountain camps, John has felt a special attraction and call to the mountains. He also enjoys hunting, fishing, camping, and being with great friends outdoors. He feels incredibly blessed to live in this wonderful part of the world that is Northwest Montana. John is passionate about his love for Glacier National Park as a true national treasure that must be protected. He is a member of the Glacier Mountaineering Society and has climbed over 50 peaks in the Park, some with multiple ascents. He continues to add to the list and loves exploring the wonders of Glacier National Park.

John is in active medical practice as an emergency physician at Kalispell Regional Medical Center. He has served in medical staff leadership at KRMC as Chief of Staff in 2008 and was Flathead County EMS Medical Director in 2006. He continues to serve as medical director of the ALERT helicopter program, which does many wilderness rescues in Northwest Montana. He has an incredible wife, Lori and three wonderful kids, Rachel, Ben and Mike, all of whom share John's love of the outdoors.

Scott Burry was born in Indiana but destined for the Rocky Mountains since his first ski trip there at the age of 10. The road getting to Montana was long but filled with valuable experience.

It included a stop in Virginia to complete an emergency medicine residency at the University of Virginia where he also became active with the U.S. Ski Patrol and completed the OEC (outdoor emergency care) course.

Scott moved to Minnesota where he practiced in an emergency medicine residency program as faculty for 3 ½ years. During this time a passion for Wilderness Medicine developed and eventually led him to Peru as a team leader on multiple occasions for medical missions along the Ucayali River.

Finally, an opportunity presented itself in the emergency room in Kalispell, Montana. Jumping at the opportunity to practice with like-minded outdoor enthusiasts he moved to Montana in 2007 and immediately started climbing peaks and diving into the backcountry. He eagerly looks forward to a future in the mountains with his wife and kids and is determined to always come back alive.

Brad Roy and his son Stuart

Brad A. Roy, and his wife Susan reside in Kalispell, where they enjoy all that the Montana outdoor has to offer, especially trekking through the backcountry of Glacier National Park. A regular runner, Brad achieved a personal best marathon time of 2:21 in 1982 while Susan prefers the slower paced hiking. Their daughter Heather is nearing completion of two bachelor degrees at Montana State University and resides in Bozeman, Montana with her husband Ron. Son Stuart also attends MSU and is an avid backpacker and enjoys backcountry photography. Stuart and Brad enjoyed a two week backpack trip in the high Sierras this past summer.

Brad serves as the Executive Director of the Summit Medical Fitness Center, a 114,800 sq. ft. medically integrated facility associated with Kalispell Regional Medical Center in Kalispell, Montana. He is a fellow in the American College of Sports Medicine and the American College of Healthcare Executives and has published numerous peer reviewed manuscripts and book chapters. Dr. Roy earned his bachelor degree in physical education from Point Loma Nazarene University and holds a master degree from San Diego State University in Exercise Physiology and a Ph.D. in clinical exercise physiology from Columbia Pacific University.

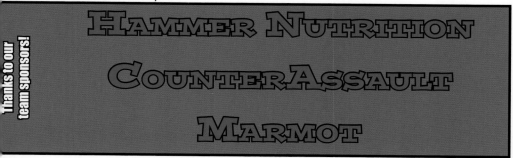

The routes presented in this climbing guidebook are all presented in the same format to help the reader locate the necessary information.

Each route is divided into a ten color-coded sections to help the reader easily follow the route, learn more about the peak, trailhead, return routes, as well as other information.

Reference Section: The first page of each section contains a photo of the mountain, statistics such as trailhead location, distance, elevation gain, and degree of difficulty. *Page 12 explains the contents of the* **Reference Section** *in more detail.*

We have provided metric conversions for each measurement.

Learn more about the peak in this section; such as, what makes this peak unique and other juicy nuggets of information. Look here to learn some history about the mountain and learn about other established routes.

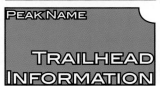

Look in this section to find the trailhead, hiking trail information, and overnight options (if any) for each peak. All mileage measurements are from the park service.

Important reminders for the trail section are in this color.

Camping information is in this color.

Read the route narrative and see illustrated route photos.

The "**CRUX**" of each climb is noted and shows how to climb through the most important section of the climb. It is designated by a black box with the fluorescent green letters. If the route

CRUX

does not have a difficult section, such as Appistoki Peak, a challenging portion route finding on the route may be designated as the "**CRUX**".

Much of the climbing in this area of the park actually requires more slogging through scree slopes than it does climbing through cliffs.

Whenever possible the route descriptions are located on the photo they describe. If not they can be found in text boxes beside the photos.

Also look for **Blue Bars** which identify the same feature in multiple photographs.

Potential problems, safety warning or dangers on the route are in this color.

Look for **Bonus Peaks** and **Bonus Routes** in this section. It is always nice to get a bonus and these bonuses are a great way to make the most of time spent in the park!

Sometimes it is only safe to descend one way.

Read instructions for descending from the peak here.

Potential problems or dangers on the return route are in this color. Heed these warnings and return safely!

PEAK NAME

OTHER OPTIONS

Check this section for side trips or other summits to fill out the day. *Remember, when climbing, that it is always further, takes longer, and is more difficult than it looks.*

Important reminders are in this color.

PEAK NAME

SUMMIT VIEWS

CHECK HERE FOR A QUOTATION ABOUT CLIMBING OR AN INTERESTING FACT ABOUT GLACIER NATIONAL PARK.

See color photographs with peak identification in this section. If you are really good with a map and compass you may be able to identify even more peaks.

PEAK NAME

ROUTE MAP

Legend:

U.S.G.S. Map: Topo Name
Contour Interval = Check Each Map
Image provided by mytopo.com
Map Produced by the U.S. Geological Service

All topo map images are used with permission from mytopo.com and produced by the U.S. Geological Survey.

National Geographic
Trails Illustrated Maps
Glacier/Waterton Lakes National Parks

Check out the topo map with trail junctions, marked route with cross-referenced coordinates to aid in completing the route.

⬡ Indicates Important Hiking Trail Waypoints

⬤ Designates GPS Route Waypoints

Check the contour interval while reading the route maps. Not all contours are the same.

PEAK NAME

ROUTE PROFILE

Elevations and distances are not exact due to variations in the chosen route.

Image provided by mytopo.com

This section provides a graph of the elevation gain over the length of the route.

Elevation profiles are provided by mytopo.com

PEAK NAME

GPS WAYPOINTS

GPS Waypoints are best used in conjunction with a compass, topo map, and common sense.

Relying solely on a GPS for navigation is NOT recommended.

Although waypoints are not exact, they are still useful in case of poor weather or to help locate the correct location on a difficult section of a route. Load them into a GPS and follow the route. We have also include UTM (Universal Transverse Mercator) coordinates for navigating short distances. *See Appendix (p. 190) for more information on GPS use.*

Z) ... Important Trail Junctions are marked alphabetically with ( ).

#] ... GPS Route Waypoints are marked with [#] ascending the route.

Compass and map reading skills are essential for traveling in the backcountry.

THE REFERENCE SECTION:

Description: What makes this peak unique or worth climbing?

Difficulty: How difficult is it to climb the peak? Numerous factors such as physical fitness and climbing ability contribute to success. Descriptions of difficulty ratings are on page 14. These are the authors' rating from their experience climbing the routes.

GMS Climb Rating: Route Ratings (p. 18) address the risk associated with a climb and skills needed to complete the route. *The GMS Climbing Rating System is used with permission.*

Time Required: How long should it take beginning to intermediate climbers to complete the route? Find out here. Remember many factors effect speed of travel.

Season: What months of the year do "normal" people climb this peak? Keep in mind that climbing is always dependent upon weather, which can change from moment to moment in the park. Experienced mountaineers have climbed many of these peaks in the off-season as well. "CLIMB GLACIER NATIONAL PARK" does **NOT** cover those approaches.

One-Way Distance: This section gives the **one-way distance** from the recommended trailhead to the summit. Exceptions are marked with * and are noted in a footnote at the bottom of the section. Off-trail distances are only estimates due to differences of approaches and route finding to the established routes.

Elevation Change: This section provides the total change in elevation from the recommended trailhead to the summit of each peak as listed on the U.S.G.S. Quad map. Exceptions are marked with ** and are noted in a footnote at the bottom of the section.

Elevation: How tall is the mount, mountain, peak, or butte?

Rank in Height: There are 234 officially named high points in Glacier National Park. Of those, 175 are named peaks and the other 59 are named points or ridges. Look here to find out where the featured peak, point, or ridge fits in that ranking. For example, 15 of 234 indicates that the peak is the 15th tallest peak in the park.

Trailhead Location: The recommended trailhead for each climb is listed first. Optional trailheads may be listed as well. The trail to the route featured in each section departs from the recommended trailhead. Trailhead information is located on pages 20 and 21.

U.S.G.S. Topo Maps: The 7.5 Minute Series Topographic Map series are listed for each peak. The first map listed will contain the peak's geographic location. It is **ALWAYS** a good idea to have a map and a route map can be found at the end of each route section. The symbols (◯ and ⬡) indicate a GPS waypoint on the map. *All maps are produced by the U.S. Geological Survey and used with permission from mytopo.com.*

Trails Illustrated Map: National Geographic Maps featuring Two Medicine (315) are recommended for reference while reaching the off-trail portion of the route.

First Recorded Ascent: If available, the first ascent party and date is listed here. Many times only one name is listed as the first ascent party but usually the peaks were climbed in groups just as they are today. After all, it is more fun that way!

THE TWO MEDICINE AND FIREBRAND PASS AREA:

Peaks in the Two Medicine and Firebrand Pass areas present a variety of options for climbing. There are few opportunities for actual technical climbing yet scrambling options abound. Perhaps the most enjoyable part of climbing in this section of the park are the extended ridges between peaks. Scree slopes interlaced with scores of wild flowers pull the eyes down to the ground while vistas with beautiful peaks rising above dark blue lakes and lush green forests flood all of the senses with their splendor.

The Two Medicine Valley is not known as a bastion for high peaks but it certainly has diversity. Trails to Firebrand, Two Medicine, Dawson and Pitamakan Passes allow climbers to quickly gain elevation to the ridge tops. The shortest peak, Never Laughs Mountain, is higher than 36 of the 50 United States high points. Rising Wolf Mountain, the tallest peak in the Two Medicine Valley, stands in as the 19th tallest peak in the park.

CLIMBER REGISTRATION:

Registration for climbing in Glacier National Park is not required; but it is highly recommended. Registering for all climbs in this guidebook can be accomplished at the Two Medicine Ranger Station prior to departing on the climb.

The Ranger Station is located at the entrance to the Two Medicine Campground. The ranger station is generally staffed from the end of May until the middle of September. The hours of operation are from 7:00 a.m. until 4:30 p.m. The phone number for the Two Medicine Ranger Station is (406) 226-4484. *If the Two Medicine Ranger Station is closed for the season a call to the Apgar Backcountry office at (406) 888-7859 is appropriate as well.* Registering for a climb ensures that the park rangers and/or rescue teams will be able to locate your party if there is a problem.

Registration is easy. Just fill out a piece of paper with your name, intended route, return time, identify safety equipment, and leave them the description of your vehicle. The rangers use the registration form to make sure you have returned. Having the vehicle information helps if you return after hours. If your car is gone, they assume the group has returned from the climb. Make sure to thank them for the great job they do in the park.

If you do register and leave a climbing itinerary with the rangers make sure to not deviate from the planned climb. It would be a bad scene to have rangers out looking for a party that was not climbing where they said they would be.

If you do register, please inform the Rangers that the party has returned as well. This can be accomplished by leaving a note at the Ranger Station.

BACKCOUNTRY PERMIT INFORMATION:

Visit **www.nps.gov/glac/planyourvisit/backcountry.htm** for all of the details on reserving a backcountry campsite as well as other useful information. A very specific process must be used to reserve a site so make sure to follow all of the steps to enjoy your time here in Glacier's backcountry.

Difficulty Ratings:

Rating the difficulty of any activity is subjective at best. In climbing this is also true!

There is a difference between climbing ratings and difficulty ratings.

Climbing Rating refers to the nature of the route and risk involved while climbing.

Difficulty Rating refers to physical exertion required during the climb. Difficulty ratings are based on the writers and their climbing team member's experiences and opinions. These climbs may be more or less difficult because of your experience and level of physical fitness.

Many elements, including past experience, training, fitness level, and mental attitude contribute to successfully summiting a peak. Having the right balance of energy (food) and hydration (water) will be a key consideration for any climb. Too much or not enough of either can ruin a great day.

There are days when all of these factors align and life is good! On the other hand, there are days when multiple factors weigh against a climber and it just is not going to be a great day. Call it what you will, but it just is not your day. Do you feel like you have to drag your body up the trail or route? Does something not feel quite right? In that case recognize it, communicate with your climbing partners and turn around.

The mountain will be waiting for you next time.

There are no superheroes in climbing.

Climb within your own ability.

The route to Bishops Cap is featured in

Climb Glacier National Park
Volume One: Logan Pass, The Garden Wall and Siyeh Bend

Purchase from a retailer or order on-line At:
www.climbglacier.com

DIFFICULTY RATINGS EXPLAINED:

PAINLESS (Well Almost)

These climbs are perfect for beginning climbers. **This is a good climb for those with a little time and patience.** Try a PAINLESS climb to see if climbing is for you.

One-way route distance is usually less than 3 miles (4.8 km) and/or total elevation gains are less than 1,500 feet (457 m).

Unfortunately there are no climbs in the Two Medicine Valley or from Firebrand Pass that are rated PAINLESS. The distance required to reach the summits is too great and elevation of the valley floor is low. *For example, Two Medicine Lake sits at 5,164 feet (1,574 m) in elevation and the lowest peak, Never Laughs Mountain, measures 7,641 feet (2,329 m) in elevation but the distance to reach the peak is nearly 5 miles (8 km).* The closest entry for PAINLESS climbs would be **Calf Robe Mountain** (p. 36) or **Red Crow Mountain** (p. 52) from Firebrand Pass. Both of these climbs require greater amounts of elevation gain and mileage but a majority of the distance and elevation are gained on hiking trails. Other options include **Scenic Point** (p. 90) and the **Two Medicine Trifecta** (p. 91).

If a **TRULY** PAINLESS climb is desired consider peaks out of VOLUME ONE: LOGAN PASS, THE GARDEN WALL, AND SIYEH BEND series of "CLIMB GLACIER NATIONAL PARK." These climb begin at a much higher elevation and require less elevation gain and travel. The peaks include **Mount Oberlin, Haystack Butte** and **Cataract Mountain**.

TOLERABLE (Sort Of)

This level of climb will physically test the body that is not properly conditioned. The key here is to be in shape before beginning to climb! Being "**Sort Of**" in shape will not cut it!

One-way route distance is usually less than 5 miles (8.0 km) and/or total elevation gains are less than 2,500 feet (762 m).

CHALLENGING (Pretty Much)

This is the route that a **Weekend Warrior** can conquer but will have sore muscles when done. There are many climbs in Glacier National Park requiring this level of exertion to reach the summit. **Do not be a Weekend Warrior.** Start an exercise plan and stick with it. Your body will thank you for it!

One-way route distance is usually less than 8 miles (12.9 km) and/or total elevation gains are less than 4,000 feet (1,219 m).

Pages 25-27 have information on physical preparation for climbing in Glacier.

ARDUOUS (Absolutely)

These routes are for all the **He-man/She-gals** out there who never quite have enough challenge. **This level of climbing demands that climbers be in top physical condition.** One way to make a climb less arduous is to make it an overnight trip.

One-way route distance is usually greater than 8 miles (12.9 km) and/or total elevation gains are usually much more than 4,000 feet (1,219 m).

Climbing In Glacier:

Mountain climbing in Glacier National Park is recognized as an acceptable activity (*your freedom to climb is provided by law*); however, the National Park Service presently designates the activity as "*not encouraged.*"

The sedimentary nature of the rock in Glacier National Park makes it brittle. Thin holds break easily. Test all hand holds and foot placements before placing the complete weight of your body on them.

Remember that different directions of pulls may dislodge a rock from its placement. Know the rocks and be certain of your safety. Do not be reckless and know your limitations as well as the limitations of those who are climbing in the group.

Every area of the park has ledges filled with scree or talus. Scree and talus are different sizes of rock deposited on the slopes from the cliff faces. The presence of scree and talus makes climbing the slopes difficult and descending on them quite enjoyable.

Do not be deceived by the photos and illustrations provided in this guide. The perspective is frequently distorted due to the angle of the photograph. This results in the correct height, grade of the slope, and distance not accurately being depicted.

An enjoyable aspect of climbing in the park is traversing along the intervening ridge top between prominent points. Once the ridge is achieved, they can generally be followed with little difficulty. If a blockage is found look on each side of the ridge for likely points that allow you to follow the route just below the ridge.

There are routes in Glacier National Park that require climbing with ropes and gear. This guidebook does not feature those routes since they are for intermediate to advanced climbers who have the proper training and equipment.

This guidebook uses the Glacier Mountaineering Society Climbing Rating system (p. 18) to rate each climb. These classifications are a **GUIDELINE** but do not take them lightly. They do not account for the climber's ability or physical health nor do they account for the current conditions of the rock in the park.

Serious injury can occur on the simplest sections of climbing or hiking trails. Take nothing for granted and always look for the safest way to climb through challenging sections of the route. **Purchase and wear a climbing helmet when climbing in areas with potential rock fall.** Protecting the brain is worth the extra weight! Wearing a helmet can prevent brain injury!

When climbing in areas with potentially loose rock exercise extreme caution. A rock can bound down gullies, couloirs, and slopes with incredible speed. Never climb above or below other climbers if there is a potential for rock fall. Be cautious and stop if you are climbing above a teammate or other climbers. Be aware of rock fall caused by freezing and subsequent thawing of water as well as falling rocks caused by mountain goats and other animals.

.

Use caution while crossing snow and ice. Approaches that require crossing snowfields that can be very dangerous. Carry an ice axe and learn how to self-arrest. Cut steps for other climbers in your party and consider belaying members of the party across sections covered with snow. None of the routes in this guidebook require glacier travel.

Traversing slopes with loose scree, rolling talus or slippery vegetation can be quite challenging. Trekking poles or an ice axe adds stability and reduces the chance of injury.

Read This Important Notice!

It is a Federal Offense to possess, destroy, deface, remove, dig, disturb natural, cultural, and archeological resources.

It is also illegal to throw, toss or roll rocks.

Preserving your park is important!

It is against the law to walk, climb, enter, ascend, descend, or traverse on an archeological or cultural resource, monument, or statue.

You also can't possess, destroy, injure, deface, remove, dig or disturb any structure or its contents, as well as other cultural or archeological resources in the park.

Oh and by the way, it is also illegal to use instruments to look for resources and artifacts.

IN OTHER WORDS ... JUST LEAVE STUFF ALONE!

Check out a portion of the Federal law below for more information!

Title 36: Parks, Forests, and Public Property

CHAPTER I: NATIONAL PARK SERVICE, DEPARTMENT OF THE INTERIOR

PART 2: RESOURCE PROTECTION, PUBLIC USE AND RECREATION

.1 - Preservation of natural, cultural and archeological resources.

a) Except as otherwise provided in this chapter, the following is prohibited:

1.) Possessing, destroying, injuring, defacing, removing, digging, or disturbing from its natural state:

i) Living or dead wildlife or fish, or the parts or products thereof, such as antlers or nests.

ii) Plants or the parts or products thereof.

iii) Nonfossilized and fossilized paleontological specimens, cultural or archeological resources, or the parts thereof.

iv) A mineral resource or cave formation or the parts thereof.

2.) Introducing wildlife, fish or plants, including their reproductive bodies, into a park area ecosystem.

3.) Tossing, throwing or rolling rocks or other items inside caves or caverns, into valleys, canyons, or caverns, down hillsides or mountainsides, or into thermal features.

4.) Using or possessing wood gathered from within the park area: Provided, however, That the superintendent may designate areas where dead wood on the ground may be collected for use as fuel for campfires within the park area.

5.) Walking on, climbing, entering, ascending, descending, or traversing an archeological or cultural resource, monument, or statue, except in designated areas and under conditions established by the superintendent.

6.) Possessing, destroying, injuring, defacing, removing, digging, or disturbing a structure or its furnishing or fixtures, other cultural or archeological resources.

7.) Possessing or using a mineral or metal detector, magnetometer, side scan sonar, other metal detecting device, or sub-bottom profiler.

Please note: Glacier National Park Climbing Classifications are unique to Glacier National Park. A Class 3 rated climb in Glacier National Park may not be the same as a Class 3 rated climb in others areas of the world.

The Glacier Mountaineering Society System (GMS):*

The GMS rating system for Glacier National Park includes the overall difficulty of the climb and designates the most difficult section of the climb by adding a number in parentheses after the Class in Roman Numeral Rating. The GMS System also rates the Round Trip Distance and Elevation Gain by using a set of S, M, or L.

Class I (1): Easy - (Trail hiking)
Class II (2): Moderate - (Low angle scrambling)
Class III (3): Difficult - (High angle scrambling, moderate cliffs, considerable exertion. A rope might be necessary for beginners)
Class IV (4): Very Difficult - (Higher angle cliffs, increased exposure. Rope required for belaying)
Class V (5): Severe - (High angle cliffs with severe exposure. Protection placed by leader. Technical climbing experience is necessary.)
Class VI (6): Extremely Severe - (Direct aid technical climbing. Overall rating in this classification reserved for only the biggest technical climbs such as the North Face of Mount Siyeh or the East Face of Mount Gould.)

<u>**Round Trip Distances**</u>

Short	1 to 6 miles
Medium	6 to 12 miles
Long	12 to 20 miles or longer**

<u>**Elevation Gain**</u>

Short	Less than 3,000 feet
Medium	3,000 to 4,500 feet
Long	Over 4,500 feet**

**Exceptional stamina is required

Consider the following examples:

A Class 2 route with the most difficult section being Class 3 with a round-trip distance of 8 miles (12.8 km) and an elevation gain of 2,800 feet (853 m) would be indicated as Class II (3) MS.

A Class 4 route with the most difficult section being Class 4 that has a round-trip distance of 14 miles (22.5 km) and 5,000 feet (1,524 m) of elevation gain is Class IV (4) LL.

* GMS Rating System used with permission from Glacier Mountaineering Society in Kalispell, MT.

For more information on the Glacier Mountaineering Society look on-line at:

www.glaciermountaineers.com

Join the Glacier Mountaineering Society and find other like-minded folks who share a passion for climbing in the park. There are also scheduled climbs throughout the year that are open to GMS members. This is a great way to learn skills and share a day in the park. **See the GMS web site for details on membership.**

CLIMBER BEWARE:

You are about to enter a realm from which you can never return. Once you are addicted to "climbing" there is no turning back. **Climbing can permanently alter your life!**

Standing on the summit of a mountain puts life in perspective. Be warned, scrambling amongst Glacier's peaks is dangerous and must not be taken lightly. One misplaced step or one loosed rock can alter a life in just a moment. Up there people die when they or others are careless.

This guidebook is not a substitute for common sense. It is not a training manual.

Are you an aspiring climber? Do these things before you climb!

Protect your brain by purchasing and wearing a climbing helmet. They are a good health insurance policy! To quote a friend, "**Climbing helmets are sexier than brain damage!**" **Educate** yourself using the resources available to you. Utilize organizations (such as local mountaineering societies/clubs or climbing stores), training workshops/programs, and books to teach basic to advanced mountaineering skills. **Locate** and climb with a group of experienced climbers. Most groups are more than willing to include a beginner in the climb as long as they are physically fit and climb safely.

Live to climb another day. Common sense and a healthy respect for the mountain go a long way while climbing in Glacier National Park. Do not take risks. There is usually more than one way to complete a route. Be patient and scout around until you find a route that is "safe" for you and your group. Remember it is **always okay** to turn around and reassess the route or even return to the trailhead.

CONSIDER THE FOLLOWING:

The WEATHER in Glacier National Park is wildly unpredictable. Check the weather before beginning the trip. **Prepare for the worst and hope for the best.** Carry rain gear on every trip, even if you are sure you will not need it! Do not risk climbing in poor weather if your group is not properly equipped. Turn back if conditions are not favorable for climbing and try another day. Carry the necessary gear *(see page 190)* to ensure your safety no matter what conditions you face, but above all use common sense.

LIGHTNING is a great hazard for climbers in Glacier's high country. Learn how to identify the risks of storms by studying the clouds and by scanning the western horizon where most of the storms originate. **If there is a risk of thunderstorms reschedule the climb.** During a climb, quickly get to the lower elevations in the trees as soon as possible if storms threaten.

INSECTS are more of a nuisance in the park than a serious threat to health. Some of the peaks in the park, such a Stanton Mountain, have healthy populations of annoying insects. **Carry bug spray if you desire.**

GRIZZLY BEARS frequent the slopes and summits of many peaks in the park. They are searching for a meal or just hanging out in the cool breeze. **Carry bear spray within reach at all times.** See **Bear Safety** *on page* 191 *for more information.*

19

The trailheads listed in this guidebook are listed from the Two Medicine Valley to Eas Glacier and finally to U. S. Highway 2. With the exception of the *Midvale Creek Trailhea* all of the trailheads have signs. There is an entrance fee that must be paid to enter the Tw Medicine Valley. There are no entrance stations at the *Lubec Lake* and *Midvale Cree Trailheads,* but make sure you carry a pass!

The Trailheads At Two Medicine

There are public restrooms near the Two Medicine Store.
Visit the store to purchase food, merchandise and cool beverages after your climb!

Scenic Point Trailhead

This trailhead is located on the west side of the road to Two Medicine. It is about 3/4 mile from the main parking area. This trailhead is well marked. There is ample parking at the trailhead.

South Shore Trailhead

The trailhead is located behind Glacier Par Boat Company's ticket kiosk. Park in th main parking area and walk to the sout past the ticket booth. Park here to catch th *Sinopah* as well.

John VanArendonk photo.
South Shore Trailhead (See description above)
Main Parking Lot and Sinopah Boat Launch
Scenic Point Trailhead (See description above)
Appistoki Creek Bridge
Restrooms and Two Medicine Store
Two Medicine Ranger Station
The Two Medicine Road leads to the trailhead at Entrance Station. This road also leads to the Looking Glass Highway.
To North Shore Trailhead (See description below)

North Shore Trailhead

To reach this trailhead drive to the Two Medicine Area and turn right at the Two Med cine Ranger Station. *You have missed the turn if you cross the Appistoki Creek bridge.* Th road leads to the Two Medicine Campground. Stay to the left at each junction and loca a parking area at the outlet end of Pray Lake where a bridge crosses the Two Medicir River. Cross the bridge and walk a short distance to the junction. The trail forks to the le or right depending upon your chosen climb for the day.

This trailhead accesses both Dawson and Pitamakan Passes.

Entrance Station

This is the trailhead for the Dry Fork Trail and an alternate route to the Pitamakan Pass Trail. This route adds additional mileage.

Park in the parking area and look for the trailhead sign on the northeast side of the entrance station.

There are no services available at this trailhead.

Midvale Creek
(East Glacier)

This trailhead is located near Glacier Park Lodge in East Glacier, Montana.

Park at the Lodge and follow the directions located in the **Dancing Lady Mountain** section (p. 44).

Purchase a BLACKFEET RECREATION PERMIT *before leaving the trailhead.*

Find the cart path next to Hole #1.

Lubec Lake

The Lubec Lake Trailhead is located along U.S. Highway 2 at mile marker #203 between East Glacier and Marias Pass. **The turn off the highway is abrupt so make sure to slow down in advance.** Park near the railroad tracks and look both ways for trains before crossing to the trailhead sign.

No services are available.

GLACIER PARK BOAT COMPANY:

The Glacier Park Boat Company was established in 1938 by Arthur J. Burch after he bought two boats in 1937 from Cap Swanson. You could say that the rest is history but that hardly does justice to the time and dedication that today's Burch family gives to their customers and their fleet of wooden boats. The entire Burch family continues to make Glacier Park Boat Company a part of their summers by living in the park, selling tickets, giving tours, performing routine maintenance, and even driving the boats. The have a lot of extra help as well! The crew at Two Medicine are knowledgeable and friendly.

The 45 foot (13.7 m) long *Sinopah* was built in 1925 - 1926 by J. W. Swanson. She carried 49 passengers on the cruise from the boat dock at Two Medicine to the upper end of Two Medicine Lake. Riding the *Sinopah* is a relaxing experience especially after a hot day of climbing or hiking in the Two Medicine Valley. If the destination is Dawson Pass or Upper

Two Medicine Lake a round-trip ticket on the *Sinopah* can cut off 6 miles (9.6 km) of trail travel. If you can time the trip right there is nothing better than knowing that as soon as you step off the boat you can head home with great memories. The view of Rising Wolf Mountain from the deck of the *Sinopah* is unique. Glacier Park Boat Company also sells one-way tokens from the head of the lake back to the parking area at Two Medicine Lake.

The *Sinopah* has invaluable historical and cultural significance. She was designed specifically for the waters in Glacier National Park to allow a smooth ride in the wind-caused waves of Two Medicine Lake. She has been a resident of the Two Medicine Valley since 1927. This wooden boat requires hours of maintenance to ensure that she is in ship-shape condition. She is truly a beautiful sight cruising on Two Medicine Lake!

Check out the Glacier Park Boat Company's web site at *www.glacierparkboats.com* for more information and the latest pricing and departure times. They serve five locations in the park. For your own ride on the *Sinopah* or one of their other boats e-mail them at *info@glacierparkboats.com*. Please make sure to include the location, date, and time desired. They also need to know the number of adults, children between ages 4 and 12, and children under the age of 4 that are going to be passengers. Make sure you leave your name, address, and a phone number so they can call you back to confirm the reservation. It is also possible to get a ride by just showing up and hoping there is room!

The cost for a round-trip ticket are: (departure times and prices are subject to change so check the web-site)
Adults $11.50   Children age 4 to 12 $5.75   Children under 4 are free

Departure times from the Two Medicine Boat Dock between July and September are:
9:00 a.m.   10:30 a.m.   1:00 p.m.*   3:00 p.m.*   5:00 p.m.

* Optional guided hiking excursions to Twin Falls are available at an additional cost
The Glacier Park Boat Company logo is used with permission from Scott and Barb Burch

22

CONDITIONING FOR GLACIER:
MOUNTAIN TREKKING AND CLIMBING CONDITIONING TIPS
BY BRAD A. ROY, PH.D., FACSM, FACHE

While venturing into the mountains and other wilderness areas can be a refreshing and exhilarating change of pace, it can easily become a painful and even dangerous experience when attempted without proper preparation and a solid base of conditioning. Mountain climbing and trekking over varied terrain with elevation changes and the added weight of a day or overnight backpack will frequently draw one's attention to areas of the body that have not been well conditioned. It is not unusual to hear comments about sore muscles that "I didn't even know I had"! Additionally, poor physical conditioning places the climber at increased risk for fatigue driven, and sometimes life-threatening, events such as falls, sprains and strains, dehydration and in rare cases, cardiac events. However, with proper conditioning people can safely enjoy challenging hiking and climbing treks with minimal discomfort.

In photo: Caleb Ballard

The key to successful conditioning is "regular exercise" or consistency over time. While the weekend warrior approach may generate some benefit, it will not provide adequate preparation for an activity as strenuous as mountain climbing. Additionally, physical exercise stimulates numerous health and conditioning benefits that persist for 2 to 48 hours post exercise and over time result in chronic conditioning and health benefits. These benefits are not realized when physical activity is sporadic. While "regular" exercise is essential so proper rest or recovery. Muscle strength adaptations occur during the repair/recovery phase; thus a 48-hour recovery period is recommended following strength sessions to allow the specific muscles challenged an opportunity to adapt.

Proper nutrition and hydration is also essential in promoting strength and endurance improvement and for maximizing energy output during a climbing adventure. Muscle primarily utilizes fat and carbohydrate to fuel exercise and the more intense the activity the more carbohydrate is utilized. Glycogen (carbohydrate) is stored by the liver (approximately 100 grams) and the muscles (400 grams) and each gram of stored glycogen holds approximately 2 grams of water. As glycogen stores are used with training and heavy exertion, water loss also occurs. Therefore, it is important to refuel glycogen stores following exercise training sessions and to maintain proper hydration during and following exercise, especially those activities of extended duration and heavy exertion, like climbing

Additionally, appropriate protein intake is necessary for muscle development following training sessions and ranges from 0.8 g/kg/day to 1.4 g/kg/day for some athletes who consistently undergo high volume/intensity training

Safe and enjoyable hiking and climbing require a strong cardiovascular base and this should be the core of your conditioning program. Start with a light to moderate intensity walking program and build to where you can handle two to three brisk walks of 30-60 minutes each week. Once you can comfortably handle the brisk walks, begin to gradually introduce varied terrain that incorporates walking up and down hills, stairs and moving across uneven surfaces. Supplement the walking program with other training devices such as elliptical trainers, stair machines, bikes and for the more fit, even jogging/running, to provide variety and an additional challenge to the leg muscles and cardiovascular system.

Scrambling and rock climbing also require muscular strength and endurance to meet the challenge of carrying a pack over varying terrain, hiking up and down hills and to better utilize the upper and lower body for climbing. Additionally, strength conditioning can help minimize the muscular soreness and discomfort that is often experienced after these invigorating outdoor adventures. Such soreness is usually associated with eccentric or negative muscular contractions where the muscle progressively lengthens against tension (e.g. quadriceps muscle activity when walking downhill or stepping off ledges)

Strength training is generally recommended three times per week, but benefits can be derived from 1-2 sessions per week. A circuit of 12-15 exercises that include both lower and upper body muscle groups, including exercises for the forearms and fingers, will stimulate an excellent base of conditioning. Resistance should be set at a level that allow

Early season climb to Mount Henry on the Mount Henry Trail.

In photo: John VanArendonk

24

or 8-12 repetitions of each exercise. This is approximately 75 percent of your maximum lifting capacity. Begin with one set of 8-12 repetitions of each exercise. While some people may choose to gradually build to 2-3 sets of each, research has shown that significant benefits are derived from a single set of each exercise. The focus should be on proper form, utilizing slow, controlled movement through the full range of motion. Because both hiking and climbing offer numerous eccentric movement challenges, slow lowering movements should be emphasized by taking 2-3 seconds to lift and 4-8 seconds to lower the resistance.

As conditioning improves and the weather allows for more outside activity, progressively increase the walking duration for one or two of the weekly walking sessions to 90 minutes or more with short day hikes. Gradually introduce a pack weighted with water bottles and other gear that adds up to approximately 1/4 - 1/3 of your body weight as a transition to outdoor hiking and mountain climbing. Adding a circuit of exercises with the weighted pack brings variety to the conditioning program, and will simulate some of the challenges experienced on the trail. Activities such as stepping up and down a step or multiple steps, stepping over logs or benches, pushups, pull-ups, squats, and other exercises can be part of a brisk outdoor walking circuit.

One of the best ways to prepare for hiking and climbing is to simulate this activity during some of the training sessions. Many fitness facilities offer climbing walls that provide an opportunity for skill/technique development and promote activity specific conditioning. Free and belayed climbing practice provides a whole body conditioning and skill development challenge. Most facilities with climbing walls also offer advice and instruction on proper climbing technique.

Changing your exercise routine and adventuring into the great outdoors can be refreshing, fun and an exhilarating way to enjoy physical activity. However, proper conditioning is essential, and should include activities that develop a strong cardiovascular base, muscular strength and endurance, and promote balance and coordination. Many fitness facilities offer exercise equipment, classes and in some centers, climbing walls that provide indoor opportunities to enhance your conditioning, especially during the winter months. Additionally, personal trainers are also available at most facilities and may be helpful to you in developing and monitoring an appropriate conditioning program that is oriented toward mountain trekking and climbing. With proper preparation you will enjoy numerous mountain treks and fond memories that will last a lifetime.

SURVIVING IN GLACIER NATIONAL PARK
BY SCOTT BURRY, M.D.

The most important part of survival is **being prepared to survive**. It is not about making traps with shoestrings or getting a spark out of a camera battery (*although those are cool skills to have and will score big points on the survival scale*). **The key to coming back alive is expecting that someday you will be thrown into a survival situation and always being ready for that day. Every time you go out.** That said, you could assemble a collection of essential survival tools that should fit in a quart zipper bag. This bag should travel with you every time you venture into the wilderness. The kit is something you have to have but will rarely need.

See the **Appendix** *for* **The Quart Bag Survival Kit** (p. 188).

Now that a nice survival kit lives in your daypack, it is time to talk about clothing. You will notice that the Quart Bag Survival Kit does not include things like "rain gear" or "base layers." Proper clothing is something you must have and will often need. If you climb enough peaks, you **WILL** get caught in the rain unexpectedly and you **WILL** get very cold if you are not ready for it.

For recommended clothing see **Equipment** (p. 188).

Another potentially lifesaving tool is a satellite-based signaling device. There are several variations on the market today with one of the most common being the products from **SPOT**. This is a relatively inexpensive device and requires a reasonable annual service fee. If you like to go solo or have a bad habit of not telling people where you are going then you should highly consider a device like this. If no one misses you, no one will come looking.

We do not recommend climbing or hiking solo, but many people do just that. Each of these scenarios based on traveling solo or in a small group. If you are in a group, as we recommend, the scenario may change slightly and the odds of survival increase exponentially. The skills needed to survive are the same but there are more people to rely upon.

YOU'RE HURT BUT NOT LOST.

Suppose it's near evening and you're on the summit of Piegan Mountain following a goat down the northwestern slope trying to nail that perfect close up. Like any aspiring photographer, you are watching your subject more than where you are going, and so it happens. You cross a larger pile of rocks when suddenly your foot slips down between two large rocks and you lose your balance, falling forward. With your foot wedged in you feel your mid shin start to lever across the top of the rock but it's too late. You cannot stop what is happening. Snap. You hit the ground screaming in pain and writhe for several minutes hyperventilating. You sit up slowly and look at your lower left leg. The sound and the pain clearly told you what has just occurred and the visual of your leg turned sideways at mid shin just confirms it. Next, a wave of nausea sweeps over you and then here it comes. All that tasty lunch is now on the ground beside you. The "Oh s##t" response now starts to kick in. "I'm on a summit!" "Nobody knows I'm up here!" "It will be dark in 2 hours!" "It's supposed to rain tonight!" **You can survive.**

Anybody that climbs knows it can be just that simple. One minute you're fine, the next you have a broken leg. **All right, do not panic.** Get your daypack off and take inventory. Go thru every pocket, every crack, and every zipper. **Your primary objective is always going to be shelter.** That said you obviously see the importance of proper clothing. Before the climb be a little paranoid and ask yourself **"Do I have clothing packed that could get me through the night?"** It is not about spending the night in comfort. Could you survive? What if it rains and you are exposed, what about a temperature drop or even snow? Grab that extra vest on the way out or even a lightweight pair of long johns just in case. The situation you now find yourself in demands that you have gear in your pack that will enable you to survive the night. Only rocks on a windblown summit surround you and if you don't have it in your pack, you're in big trouble. There aren't a lot of fancy survival tricks in this scenario but sometimes that's just the way it is. **You have be prepared, every time.**

YOU'RE LOST BUT NOT HURT.

Your goal for the week was absolute obscurity and solitude. Following that mind-set, your group decides to venture off the trail and head cross-country. The first day went reasonably well except that battering in the undergrowth. According to very rough calculations, you should have hit the trail in the adjacent valley by now, but for some reason it hasn't materialized yet. By mid afternoon, you consult the general park overview map ripped from an old hiking guidebook and realize there's not much detail there, to say the least. A compass would be nice but unfortunately, it's on the dash of your friend's car. For some reason you've completely disengaged your brain getting into this situation but if you want to get out, now is the time to turn it on.

Here are some questions that will help you decide what to do.
1) Who knows you are here?
2) When will the group be officially overdue?
3) Does anybody know where you are?
4) If you did tell someone where you were going, are you in that spot?
5) What gear do you have and how many days can you survive?
6) Is the group prepared for the current weather or what may be coming?
7) Can you reasonably expect a rescue in your situation or are you completely on your own?

Now it's decision time, do you stay or do you go?

Well, that depends on your answers to the above questions. You may have heard that you always "stay put" in a situation like this. However, if no one knows where you were going

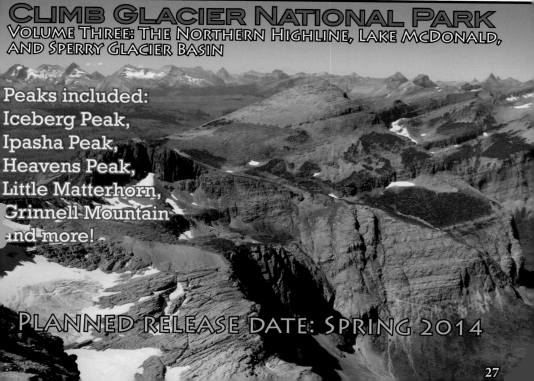

CLIMB GLACIER NATIONAL PARK
VOLUME THREE: THE NORTHERN HIGHLINE, LAKE MCDONALD, AND SPERRY GLACIER BASIN

Peaks included:
Iceberg Peak,
Ipasha Peak,
Heavens Peak,
Little Matterhorn,
Grinnell Mountain
and more!

PLANNED RELEASE DATE: SPRING 2014

and no one is going to miss you for a week, then you had better get moving. If you're lost then widen your scope. You may not know exactly where you are but in general, you will likely have an idea of your overall location. Take what you know and narrow it down as far as you can. For example, "I'm in the northwest corner of the park." "The Flathead River is to my west." "The trail I came in on was north of Logging Lake." Pick a direction and stick with it. Do not wander aimlessly; use a distant peak as a landmark and head for it. If you know there is a boundary, for example a river to the west, then head for what you know. **Try to use things you know for certain to navigate, not just "I think it's this way."** If it's getting dark, the sooner you come to grips with spending the night out the better. Use the light you have left and get busy making a fire and getting shelter. Your **Quart Bag Survival Kit** will help do these things. I hope you packed it!

YOU SIMPLY RUN OUT OF DAYLIGHT OR ENERGY TO GET WHERE YOU NEED TO BE.

In Glacier National Park, it is easy to bite off more than you can chew!

The peak that looks like it's "just right over there" might easily be miles away and several require climbing thousands of vertical feet. It wouldn't be unheard of to find yourself 30 minutes from sunset and still miles away from where you need to be. If you're backpacking with a tent then it's no big deal. If you have to throw down, just do it. If you're just out with a daypack then that's another story. **If you find yourself here, then ask yourself these questions.** "Can I for sure find my way in the dark?" "Can I rally and make it to where I need to be if I just rest and eat a little?" "What weather is expected tonight and am I ready for it?" Obviously, if snow is coming in and you're in shorts you have a problem. I hope you've realized by now that if you don't have the right gear and some survival supplies then you don't belong in the backcountry. This scenario is easy if you're prepared and can even be fun. Just get out your survival blanket and make a shelter. Make an insulating layer out of gear, make a fire, and settle in like an old cowboy. This is just part of the deal.

SEVERE WEATHER MOVES IN QUICKLY AND NOW YOU'RE STUCK.

You've bagged the peak and now you're heading home. Unfortunately, you still have 1 miles on the trail, you are exhausted, and a storm is bearing down on top of you. The temperature is dropping somewhat and it will be dark in 1 hour.

What should you do? Do you pound it down the trail just trying to get out o do you hunker down and wait it out? Well, that depends on the gear you have i your pack. If you have good rain gear and the energy to motor out then that's probably th

The Ole Creek Drainage from Calf Robe Mountain Route.

est decision. If you're not ready for rain and you're looking at 10 miles soaking wet with a dropping temperature then hypothermia is a real risk. It's a tough decision but you may be better off forming a quick shelter and staying dry. If you think a night out may be coming take what little daylight you have left and get yourself settled into a place where you can feel safe and with as much protection from the elements as possible. Whether you stay or go is situation dependent according to what you have available but if you have your quart bag survival kit, at least you have some options.

CONCLUSION:

We didn't talk a lot about survival specifics or have "how to" examples. That is a book all by itself. For a good carry-along resource try to find **The Don't Die Out There Deck**. In addition to having a deck of playing cards along to pass time on a rainy day, this set of cards has survival essentials and techniques, basic first aid information, and recommendations for helping injured colleagues. It is produced by The Mountaineers Books and can be ordered at **www.mountaineersbooks.com** or purchased in a park book store.

Sometimes staying alive is about getting lucky. If that's your plan then please stay home. You don't have to be a grizzled, leathery-faced, backwoods veteran to survive but you do have to be prepared. **If you always travel with the proper clothing and survival gear then you can go out with confidence and a sense of true freedom.** You can bag that peak and in the back of your mind, you'll know that you're equipped for the unexpected. **Do it for your family. Do it for yourself.**

EMERGENCIES IN GLACIER NATIONAL PARK:
BY JOHN VANARENDONK, M.D.

Beautiful and Potentially Dangerous: Glacier National Park is truly a gem; there is a good reason why it is "The Crown of the Continent." While roads probe the boundaries of the park and trails access the interior, Glacier National Park remains a vast, magnificent wilderness. **This unspoiled wilderness makes it beautiful and potentially dangerous.** Many places in the park are miles and hours away from any kind of help. In Glacier we are only visitors, and anyone who would go there must consider its remoteness and inaccessibility.

In 23 years of medical practice in Northwest Montana, I have treated many patients with wilderness-related illness and injuries. A common thread that runs through many of these incidents is the victim's failure to consider "what could happen." From a hiker dehydrated by running out of water on a hot day to the climber who took an unknown route of a peak, got "cliffed out," then fell and was injured, many of these incidents were the result of poor planning and could have been avoided by being prepared and following a few rules. Consider the following suggestions before ascending one of Glacier's peaks. Know what to do if an emergency occurs and understand what resources are available.

PREPARATION IS THE KEY:

One of the most important things you can do in preparation for a climb is to research the intended route. This book is a good place to start. Understanding the distance, elevation gain, off-trail bushwhacking, and other obstacles is critical to knowing what you are get ting into and knowing whether you are physically able to do the climb. Study topograph maps, look at Google Earth, and read route descriptions to gain invaluable informatio for a successful climb and to avoid mishaps. A GPS is a good tool to have but is not a ways reliable, due to varying signal reception, and should not be the sole navigation too However, laying down GPS tracks on a climb can be very valuable when clouds roll in an retracing your steps is nearly impossible. Perhaps the best resource is to go with someor who has already climbed the peak.

CLIMBING SOLO OR IN A GROUP:

When climbing, the safest situation is to climb with at least one other person and prefe ably 3-5 people who climb close together to avoid kicking rocks down on each other. climber who charges ahead and above the group risks launching rock missiles down th slope. **Climbing solo has its rewards, but one must understand that the risk increase exponentially.** A relatively minor injury such as an ankle fracture could result in death the climber is immobilized, is away from any cell signal, and hidden from rescuers. Wit no one to go for help, that climber will die of exposure and starvation. Such a scenar occasionally happens.

Climbers have been killed by climber-caused rock fall. In the event of a sickness or injur someone can stay with the victim and others who can go for help. It is important to iden tify who the driver in the group is and where they have stored the vehicle's keys, especial if the driver loses consciousness for some reason.

COMMUNICATION IN THE BACKCOUNTRY:

Carrying cell phones in the backcountry may lead to a false sense of security and th is certainly true in the park. They can be useful at higher elevations but on many peak there is no signal. Climbers must understand that they most likely will not be able to ca for help if they get in trouble. Satellite emergency locators, such as **SPOT**, are also useft

Walkie-talkies can be a very useful communication tool for a group of climbers, esp cially larger groups. Often, a group will split up for a variety of reasons. Some climb fast than others, while others may want to take a different route. **There is nothing more age nizing than having split from a climbing member with plans to meet later and the have that member not show up.** Making plans to "check in" on the radio every half ho keeps everyone in contact and knowing each other's position on the mountain. The safe way to climb is a group of 3 to 5 members who stick together.

WHAT TO THROW IN YOUR PACK:

Packing your backpack is somewhat of an art form. On the one hand, pack as light possible to avoid wasting energy carrying extra weight up a mountain. **On the other, yo need to carry all the essential equipment, hydration, and nutrition to accomplish th climb.** Everyone is a little different in how to approach this task but there are a few e sential things to consider.

The concept of layering clothing and having waterproof gear is essential. What you choo to wear depends on weather, time of year, expected terrain, and personal preference. T idea is to maintain as normal a body temperature as possible. If you are too hot, you w sweat more and therefore require more water to carry (which is heavy) to prevent deh dration. For example, when starting out on a cold morning long sleeves and pants may e needed but be ready to strip down to loose fitting (to prevent chafing) shorts and tee shirt if needed to limit sweating during strenuous uphill climbs. Well tested and broken-in waterproof hiking/climbing boots are very important as well to prevent blisters.

Always carry rain gear in your backpack (you can wear these in the morning starting out). This equipment may save your life. Many climbers start out on a warm sunny day and end up drenched in a chilly afternoon shower or snowstorm. The quickest way for a climber to become hypothermic is to be wet with exposure to the wind. **Most serious climbers have set of this gear that "lives" in their backpack and never leaves.** In truth, most climbers will be using this equipment on every climb. Even on sunny days, after rest at the summit, the body begins to cool and hypothermia becomes a possibility. Pulling on a rain shell acts as a windbreak and when combined with a base layer, it is quite warm. Often, only shell is needed before beginning the descent. Having a set of gloves is also a good idea.

All of the climbs described in this book are single-day trips, so most climbers take a lunch, and some snacks after having had a good, but not-too-heavy breakfast. Pack extra food as an emergency measure. Energy bars and trail mix are good emergency foods that tend to keep well. *See* **Appendix** (p. 188) *for recommended* **Equipment** *and* **The Quart ag Survival Kit** *for essential gear.*

HYDRATION IN THE MOUNTAINS:

This is a vital consideration in the backcountry. Most backpacks have a reservoir bladder for water with a tube coming over the shoulder to access water on the move without having to stop and get out a water bottle. If you do not have a backpack with this type of system, get one. Most of these bladders carry 2-3 liters of water and this is usually enough water to carry for the climbs described in this book, especially if you manage your body temperature as described above. Longer hikes and climbs take more planning. Sometimes this means carrying additional water. A less strenuous solution is to carry a water filter pump or purification tablets and get water from a stream. **Although not universally recommended, many climbers drink directly from the streams in the park and have used these water sources for years with no ill effects.** Giardia is a water-borne parasite that can infect you by drinking out of streams. These cases are fairly rare in Glacier. The higher in elevation a water source, the cleaner it will tend to be. If you run out of water and are getting dehydrated, drink out of a stream if it is available. The potential risk of Giardia is less than the actual, real risk of dehydration. Giardia is treatable with medication, dying from dehydration is not.

IN CASE OF EMERGENCY:

There are patterns of illness and injury that happen to climbers. There can be falls resulting in a variety of injuries including head and extremity injuries that prevent mobility.

A panoramic view from Running Eagle Falls.

One good way to prevent head injuries is to wear a climbing helmet. Exhaustion from getting lost, not having enough food, or not being physically fit is a concern. Dehydration as discussed above can lead to emergencies. Exposure to the elements from inadequate clothing can lead to hypothermia and be very dangerous. **Hopefully, planning and being prepared as discussed above will prevent this from happening but sometimes, despite doing everything "right," incidents still happen and you need to think about the possibility of being stranded on the mountain.** If the climber has no medical knowledge, taking a first aid or CPR course is advisable. In reality, apart from maintaining someone's airway, stopping bleeding, and splinting an extremity, there is not much to do in the field without supplies and equipment.

Survival success depends on five basic human needs: water, food, heat, shelter, and spiritual (will to survive, reason to live). Address each area by planning and being prepared.

EMERGENCY MEDICAL RESPONSE SYSTEM:

When you need help, there are resources within the park and in the surrounding counties. As medical director for the ALERT Helicopter program in Kalispell, Montana, I have been involved in rescues in the park borders for many years. The surrounding EMS communities have a good, cooperative relationship with the park and continue to update and coordinate services.

When an emergency occurs in the backcountry of Glacier, the first step is to notify park rangers. There are usually rangers at Visitors Centers and Ranger Stations during hours of operation. All of the lodges, such as Lake McDonald Lodge, should be able to access park rangers during off hours. Glacier National Park is a federal park and the rangers have jurisdiction and responsibility for rescues. The rangers are linked by radio throughout the park and have their own dispatch center. Rangers vary in medical certification from First Responder to Paramedic.

If there is a cell phone signal, dialing 911 will contact either Flathead County EMS or Glacier County EMS, depending on your location, which can then dispatch a ranger. Sometimes those who go for help must still drive some distance before they can contact help. It is important to identify who the driver in the group is and where they have stored their vehicle's keys, especially if the driver loses consciousness for some reason.

Rangers can request county resources to help with a response based on their on-site evaluation or from the story of a climber who has come back for help. The type of response depends on the location and the complaint, whether it's chest pain/shortness of breath, head injury, leg fracture, etc. Ground ambulances often respond to transport patients once evacuated from the backcountry. Three Rivers ambulance out of Columbia Falls evacuates patients on the west side and transports to either North Valley Hospital in Whitefis

A panoramic view from Rising Wolf Mountain.

r Kalispell Regional Medical Center based on the type of problem or patient preference. On the east side, Browning or Cutbank ambulance transports patients to their hospitals. Browning ambulance will transport and stabilize any emergency patient, but the hospital n Browning is a Federal IHS (Indian Health Service) hospital and will only keep non-tribal members long enough to stabilize and then be transferred to a community hospital. Consequently, some patients transfer to Cutbank or Kalispell.

When there is a time-sensitive threat to life or limb, the rangers will on occasion request aeromedical transport of a victim. The ALERT Helicopter program out of Kalispell Regional Medical Center has been in existence for 35 years and done many rescues in the park. The crew brings state-of-the-art Advanced Life Support capability to the field. If a climber is injured or stranded on a mountain, the rangers will get them to a suitable landing zone and the patient will be air transported to Kalispell.

n the past, ALERT did short haul, static line rescues off the side of mountains in situations when it was not safe to move a patient. A change in F.A.A. rules has halted this practice. ALERT hopes to obtain a twin-engine helicopter in the next few years that would allow the return of this service. Helicopters out of Canada and Military helicopters from Malmstrom Air Force Base in Great Falls can do short hauls and have assisted in rescues.

He who risks little, gains little. **Climbing mountains can be risky, but the rewards of reaching the summit of a peak on a clear day are difficult to describe to those who have not done it.** Pictures never do it justice. Those visual rewards are wonderful but temporary. The real reward comes from the camaraderie with fellow climbers and the knowledge you gain about yourself. There is nothing like standing in a parking lot and looking at the peak you just climbed; totally amazed that you did it. It is instructive in life to realize that sometimes you can do things you never thought you could.

Happy climbing and be safe!

A panoramic view from Chief Lodgepole Peak.

GLACIER NATIONAL PARK

A PLACE WHERE HEAVEN TOUCHES EARTH AFFORDING BRIEF GLIMPSES INTO THE WONDERS OF CREATION.

Calf Robe Mountain

FIREBRAND PASS ROUTE

Photo taken from the Lubec Lake Trailhead.

A GREAT PEAK FOR BEGINNERS IN AN ISOLATED PORTION OF THE PARK

Difficulty: Tolerable, due to trail mileage
GMS Climb Rating: Class II(3) LS
Time Required: 5-7 hours
Season: June to October
One-way Distance: 6.3 miles / 10.1 km
Elevation Change*: 2,840 feet / 865 m

Elevation: 7,920 ft / 2,414 m
Rank in Height: 173 of 234
Trailhead: Lubec Lake
U.S.G.S. Topo Map: Squaw Mountain
Trails Illustrated Map: Two Medicine 31
First Ascent: Unknown

* Elevation Change From Trailhead On Featured Route

Date Climbed: _____
Climbed With: _____
Notes: _____
_____
_____
_____
_____
_____
_____
_____

The experience of climbing in the Firebrand Pass area of Glacier National Park presents a stark contrast to climbing along the Going-to-the-Sun Highway. **Just Park and Climb!** There are no entrance stations or long lines waiting to catch a glimpse of a mountain goat. No traffic jams, no season-long road construction, or stressing to find a parking spot at Logan Pass or Siyeh Bend. No motor coaches or shuttles and best of all no crowds!

Calf Robe Mountain is part of the Lewis and Clark Range and is located approximately 5 miles northeast of Marias Pass in the southwestern portion of Glacier National Park. The Continental Divide passes over the summit and shortly afterwards makes an abrupt turn northward at Bearhead Mountain where it runs through the entirety of Glacier National Park to just north of Browns Pass at the International Border with Canada.

Firebrand Pass was called "The Bad Road" by the Blackfeet because of the dangers associated with this pass which served as a corridor between two tribe's territories.

Its present day name is associated with a 1910 fire that was reportedly started when a firebrand, a piece of burning wood, was blown across the pass moving the blaze from the Railroad Creek Drainage into the Ole Creek Drainage.

The route crosses some spectacular habitat for elk, Rocky Mountain sheep, mountain goats as well as deer. This area is also home to black and grizzly bears.

Calf Robe Mountain, Firebrand Pass, and Red Crow Mountain.

The *Lubec Lake Trailhead* (p. 21) is located on U.S. Highway 2 at mile marker #203 between East Glacier and Marias Pass. **This is a very abrupt turn-off so slow down and be cautious.**

Find a good place to park, gear up and strap on your bear spray. Cross the railroad tracks and look for the opening in the fence and the trail mileage sign. Follow the Coonsa Trail for 1.4 miles (2.2 km) to the Autumn Creek Trail Junction. Hike north (*right fork*) for 1 mile (1.6 km) to the Firebrand Pass Junction. Follow the Firebrand Pass trail (*left fork*) for 2.4 miles (3.8 km) to Firebrand Pass.

Trillium after a spring rain.

CALF ROBE MOUNTAIN

ROUTE INFORMATION

The Firebrand Pass Trail climbs through an alpine basin to the pass. A sharp eye might spot an elk or mountain goat in the basin.

Snow on the trail   Firebrand Pass

Be cautious if there is snow on the trail as seen in this photo.

Cross carefully or traverse above or below it on a safe route

Be cautious when descending through the cliffs. There are a few goat trails leading back to the pass.

There are many possible routes to this summit.

CRUX

View from a ridge off of Red Crow Mountain.

A

Firebrand Pass.

Study the route through the cliffs on the east slope of Calf Robe Mountain from Firebrand Pass. Climbers can also skirt the cliffs on the talus fields but the footing is loose. It is much more enjoyable to descend on the loose talus than it is to climb through it! Climbing near the face of the cliff occasionally offers better footing on the rocks.

A closer look at the lower section of the route

PLEASE PRACTICE THE 7 PRINCIPLES OF LEAVE NO TRACE:

Climb towards the horizon.

Above the cliffs almost 300 feet of semi-loose scree waits!

This is the most challenging portion of the route.

The scree is more stable further up the slope. The angle of the slope decreases as the summit is approached.

Continue through the scree fields. Use the breaks around the cliffs to quickly gain elevation and reduce the amount of talus you must climb through.

The route gets easier above this point.

Summit Mountain from the Calf Robe summit.

The cairn is easy to find on this scree-covered summit.

Bonus Route: The Northeast Ridge Route

The route leaves the Autumn Creek Trail nearly 1/3 mile (0.5 km) from the Lubec Lake Trail junction in a large meadow. This is really the first place where hikers get a decent view of Calf Robe Mountain after leaving the trailhead. See photo below.

The route is located just beyond a marshy area where the trail has been built up with gravel and small logs. Just beyond this built-up section the trail enters the large meadow and the off-trail portion begins.

The southeast side of Calf Robe Mountain can be accessed anywhere between the junction and the meadow but the recommended way does not require a lot of bushwhacking. See map of page 40 for route details.

Climb up the slope through the lower and upper cliffs to the rounded summit of Calf Robe. There are many options for this route. Climbing is rated Class II (3) if a safe route is found. Total distance is 4.25 miles (6.8 km). Total elevation gain is 3,030 feet (923 m) and looses 293 feet (89 m).

CALF ROBE MOUNTAIN
RETURN ROUTE

Climbing to Calf Robe from Firebrand Pass.

In photo: Tom Berquist

Descend via the same route.

Make sure you do not follow the trail into the Ole Creek Drainage if your goal is to return to the *Lubec Lake Trailhead* (p. 21)**.**

At the junction of the Firebrand Pass Trail and the Autumn Creek Trail turn south (right) and follow the trail back to the junction of the Coonsa Trail. At that junction, turn southeast (left) and follow the trail back to the *Lubec Lake Trailhead.*

CALF ROBE MOUNTAIN
OTHER OPTIONS

1) <u>Summit Mountain</u>, which stands at 8,770 feet (2,673 m) in elevation, can be reached from Calf Robe Mountain via a goat trail along the northwest side of the Continental Divide. **This is a challenging intermediate to advanced route.**

2) Climbers who are fit can accomplish traveling between Firebrand Pass and the *Scenic Point Trailhead* (p. 21) in the Two Medicine Valley in a day from either starting point.

Traversing to the saddle between Red Crow and Bearhead.

In photo: John VanArendonk

The route accesses Apistoki Peak (p. 90), an unnamed peak, Mount Ellsworth (p. 68), Bearhead Mountain (p. 60) (pictured below) and Red Crow Mountain (p. 50). See p. 58-59 for details on this great traverse.

3) Intermediate to advanced climbers can also reach **Dancing Lady Mountain** (p. 42) from this area via a ridge walk from the saddle north of Red Crow Mountain. See the **Red Crow Mountain** and **Dancing Lady Mountain** *page for the standard route approaches.*

4) A long day trip, with a two-day trip being much more enjoyable, down the Ole Creek Drainage to the trailhead at the <u>Walton Ranger Station</u> could prove entertaining. Make sure you have a campsite reserved at <u>Ole Lake</u> before leaving for this overnight trip.

1) Leave What You Find

A MAN DOES NOT CLIMB A MOUNTAIN WITHOUT BRINGING SOME OF IT AWAY WITH HIM AND LEAVING SOMETHING OF HIMSELF UPON IT. — SIR MARTIN CONWAY

Battlement, Caper, Grizzly, Rockwell, Helen, Flinsch

Do your part to preserve the park.
Don't commit a Federal Offense!
See page 17

Grizzly, Rockwell, Flinsch, Red Crow, Rising Wolf, Bearhead

In photo: Tom Berquist

2) Properly Dispose of Waste

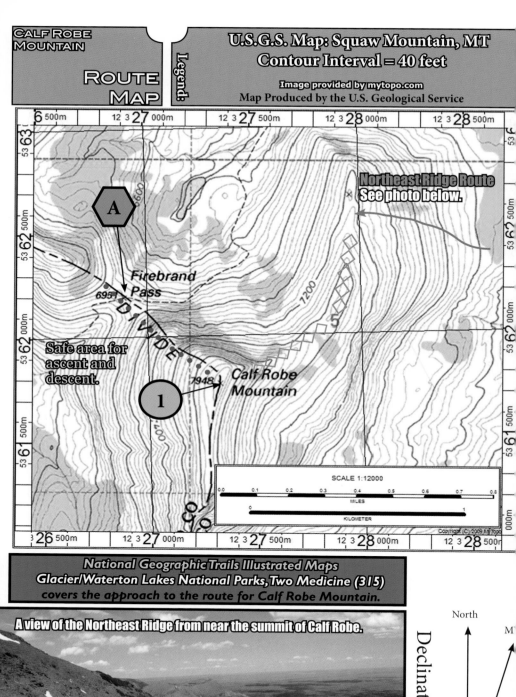

CALF ROBE
MOUNTAIN

ROUTE
MAP

Legend:

U.S.G.S. Map: Squaw Mountain, MT
Contour Interval = 40 feet

Image provided by mytopo.com
Map Produced by the U.S. Geological Service

A

Northeast Ridge Route
See photo below.

Firebrand Pass

6957

DIVIDE

Safe area for
ascent and
descent.

1

7948

Calf Robe Mountain

SCALE 1:12000

MILES

KILOMETER

Copyright (C) 2009 MyTopo

National Geographic Trails Illustrated Maps
Glacier/Waterton Lakes National Parks, Two Medicine (315)
covers the approach to the route for Calf Robe Mountain.

A view of the Northeast Ridge from near the summit of Calf Robe.

North

M

Declination

MN 14.41° E

ROUTE PROFILE

Elevations and distances are not exact due to variations in the chosen route.

Image provided by mytopo.com

Total elevation change from Firebrand Pass to Calf Robe Mountain summit: 997 feet (303 m) and the total distance is .50 miles (0.8 km).

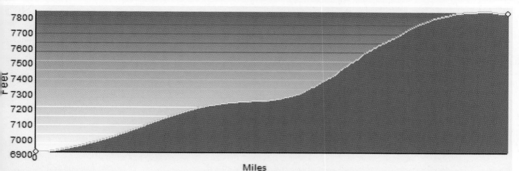

CALF ROBE
MOUNTAIN

GPS WAYPOINTS

GPS Waypoints are best used in conjunction with a compass, topo map, and common sense.

Relying solely on a GPS for navigation is NOT recommended.

	Latitude	Longitude	Elevation (ft/m)
Lubec Lake Trailhead (p. 21)	48.37176	-113.27964	5,098/1,554
UTM	12 0331 216E	53 59 916N	NAD27
Autumn Creek Junction	48.37959	-113.30549	5,485/1,671
UTM	12 0329 286E	53 60 841N	NAD27
Firebrand Pass Trail Junction	48.39211	-113.30449	5,518/1,681
UTM	12 0329 402E	53 62 231N	NAD27
A) Firebrand Pass	48.39110	-113.33820	6,951/2,118
UTM	12 0326 903E	53 62 194N	NAD27
1] Calf Robe Mountain	48.38738	-113.33213	7,948/2,414
UTM	12 0327 339E	53 61 767N	NAD27

Northeast Ridge

Calf Robe Mountain from the Lubec Lake Trailhead.

SOUTHEAST RIDGE ROUTE

Photo taken from the route.

CLIMB GLACIER NATIONAL PARK'S EASTERN-MOST SUMMIT.

Difficulty: Tolerable, due to trail mileage
GMS Climb Rating: Class (II)3 MS
Time Required: 5-7 hours
Season: June to October
One-way Distance: 5.5 miles / 8.8 km
Elevation Change*: 2,530 feet / 771 m

Elevation: 7,333 ft / 2,235 m
Rank in Height: 202 of 234
Trailhead: Midvale Creek
U.S.G.S. Topo Map: Squaw Mountain
Trails Illustrated Map: Two Medicine 31
First Recorded Ascent: Unknown

* Elevation Change From Trailhead On Featured Route

Date Climbed: _____
Climbed With: _____
Notes: _____
_____
_____
_____
_____
_____

Dancing **Lady Mountain** received a new name a few years ago. This is not a bad thing. Once called "Squaw Mountain", this peak now wears a new shiny name to match its shining position as one of Glacier National Park's eastern-most summits. The word "squaw" is a derogatory term to Native Americans and the Federal Government changed the name.

Dancing Lady's position near the eastern border allows her to stand out when viewed from Glacier Park Lodge in East Glacier, Montana. From her summit the grass-filled plains of Central Montana fade into the horizon and the peaks in the National Forests shimmer on sunny days. The Sweet Grass Hills near Cut Bank, Montana can also be seen.

Although the National Park Service lists the northern summit of Dancing Lady Mountain as 7,333 feet, the southwestern summit is 20 feet higher. Take the time and stand on both of them. It takes just a little more effort to reach both points.

There are two trailheads that can be used to reach Dancing Lady Mountain. The most direct is on the *Autumn Creek Trail* from the *Midvale Creek Trailhead*.

The route could also be reached by an extended hike from *Lubec Lake Trailhead* (p. 21).

DANCING LADY MOUNTAIN

TRAILHEAD INFORMATION

If choosing the *Midvale Creek Trailhead* (p. 21 & 44) make sure each member of the group purchases a Blackfeet Use Permit prior to departing from the trailhead.

A **Blackfeet Use Permit** costs around $10.00 and can be found at most stores that sell fishing and hunting licenses in the area.

The *Autumn Creek Trail* is part of the *Continental Divide Trail System*. This particular section of the trail passes through tribal land from the Midvale Creek Road to the park boundary. The "trail" to the park boundary is actually a combination of single-track and "road." *See Trailhead directions on page 44 and the top map on page 48.*

Many of the "roads" leading from Montana 49 to the park boundary are poor at best and at certain times of the year are absolutely impassable. Deep ruts in the "road" would require high-clearance four-wheel drive to successfully reach to the park boundary. The total distance for this route is 5.5 miles (8.8 km) and has an elevation gain of 2,761 feet (841 m).

It is best to walk from the "trailheads" on the eastern side of Glacier and enjoy the views!

Photo of Dancing Lady Mountain taken from Medicine.

DANCING LADY MOUNTAIN

FINDING THE TRAILHEAD

1

After parking (leave plenty of room for guests and staff), locate the golf course behind the lodge. Follow the cart path down the hill to the gate below Hole #1.

2

Walk down Midvale Creek Road over the bridge then past a brown building. Hike up the road until you see a 15 m.p.h. sign. The next right (first) leads past a shack (3) and the next right (second) leads to the correct forest track (4).

3 Falling down shack Second right turn

The Autumn Creek Trail begins here.

4

Look for orange tags on the trees.

5

Take the first left!

(4) The **KEY** to locating the correct track/trail is to **take the left fork at each junction** (5) after passing the shack and <u>second</u> right turn. At times the correct path is a road and sometimes it is a single-track trail.

DANCING LADY MOUNTAIN

ROUTE INFORMATION

Occasional views of Dancing Lady confirm the correct track. It is 2.1 miles (3.5 km) to the park boundary from photo (3).

Dancing Lady Mountain is seen while walking along the forest roads.

Look for orange trail markers along the Autumn Creek Trail.

A sign indicates the park boundary which is well marked.

AUTUMN CREEK TRAIL

EAST GLACIER R. S.   3.5 Km ð
LUBEC TRAILHEAD   11 Km ð
OLE LAKE   16 Km ð
SUMMIT - MARIAS PASS 21 Km ð

CAMPING PERMIT REQUIRED

1

Don't step in fresh grizzly scat!

The wide-forest road continues for some distance into the park.

This road is closed to bicycles and vehicles.

Eventually the wide-forest road turns into a single-track trail.

A current key to locating the start of the off-trail portion of the route is to find the tree with barbed-wire stapled into the bark. This tree is a DNA collecting site for Grizzly population study.

When the study ends the wire will be gone, but the tree will still show scars from the wire.

CRUX

The off-trail portion begins on the single-track section of the trail about 1 mile from the end of the wide-forest road.

If the trail begins to descend down a long hill you have missed the route!

2

Walk about 115 paces past the barbed-wire stapled tree and look for the trail. It is usually marked with flagging at start of the route. The color of the flagging may change!

After about 1/4 mile (0.4 km) the route breaks out into the open. Follow the ridge towards the summit!

3

Remember this cairn for the return route.

Climb to the obvious rocks along the ridge. If you want to walk to the ridge on the north Woman Standing Alone can be seen. A Class V climb is required to reach the top of the pinnacle. There is a rappel station just below the top of the pinnacle.

In photos: Rod Graham

Woman Standing Alone

There is some climbing on loose Class II rocks along the ridge. If you want some less-than enjoyable Class II scree there is plenty of that also!

The summit

4

The summit cairn is located on top of the scree-covered knob. Take some time and explore the ridge-line to the south-west as well.

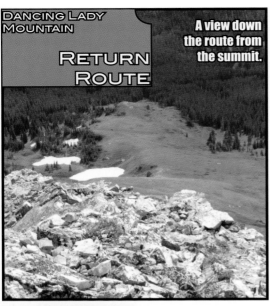

DANCING LADY MOUNTAIN

RETURN ROUTE

A view down the route from the summit.

Descend the scree slopes from the true summit of Dancing Lady Mountain.

Route finding through the trees is much easier by following the game trail.

Return to the *Midvale Creek Trailhead* (p. 21).

Take a some extra time to explore the unique pillar formation now referred to as "Woman Standing Alone" before heading back to the forest floor. **Bring climbing gear to reach the top of this formation it is a technical climb.** The name "Woman Standing Alone" is quite descriptive of what many Blackfeet women did as they stood alone and waited the return of their husbands from battle or raids.

DANCING LADY MOUNTAIN

OTHER OPTIONS

1) Dancing Lady Mountain is on an isolated ridge extending from the Continental Divide. It is possible to spend the day exploring the north and south sides of the ridge or if you are confident with route finding walk along the ridge to a saddle between **Red Crow Mountain** (p. 50) and **Bearhead Mountain** (p. 60). After reaching the saddle climb up the loose scree to the summit of Red Crow Mountain and follow the return route directions from there to the Firebrand Pass - Autumn Creek Trail Junction. At that junction turn left (north) and return to the *Midvale Creek Trailhead* (p. 21). This could be a long day if any of the group is unfit!

2) This could be an enjoyable point-to-point trip with a little pre-planning and another vehicle at the *Lubec Lake Trailhead* (p. 21). Instead of turning left at the Firebrand Pass - Autumn Creek Trail Junction turn right and hike to the next trail junction. At the Coonsa Trail Junction turn left (southeast) and walk to the *Lubec Lake Trailhead*.

Returning to the Firebrand Pass Trail from Lena Lake.

In photo: John VanArendonk and Read Vaughan

3) Lena Lake can be reached from this ridge but requires some persistence as well as route finding through some cliffs. After reaching the lake a bushwhack would be necessary to reach the Firebrand Pass Trail. This could be an incredible day for groups with excellent route finding skills.

DANCING LADY MOUNTAIN

SUMMIT VIEWS

THE PARK'S AVERAGE JULY TEMPERATURE IS 79° FAHRENHEIT. THE LOWEST AVERAGE TEMPERATURE IS 15° FAHRENHEIT IN FEBRUARY.

Calf Robe, Summit, Little Dog, Firebrand Pass, Red Crow

Red Crow, Bearhead, Ellsworth

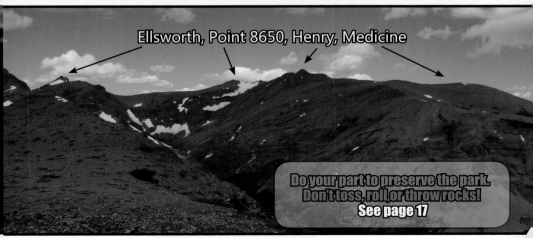

Ellsworth, Point 8650, Henry, Medicine

Do your part to preserve the park. Don't toss, roll, or throw rocks!

See page 17

6) Minimize Campfire Impacts

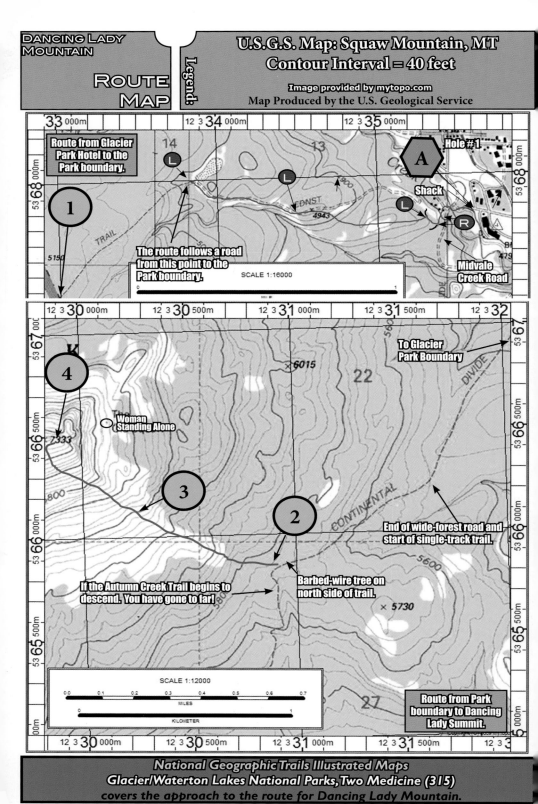

DANCING LADY MOUNTAIN

ROUTE MAP

Legend:

U.S.G.S. Map: Squaw Mountain, MT
Contour Interval = 40 feet

Image provided by mytopo.com
Map Produced by the U.S. Geological Service

Route from Glacier Park Hotel to the Park boundary.

Hole #1

A

Shack

The route follows a road from this point to the Park boundary.

SCALE 1:16000

Midvale Creek Road

To Glacier Park Boundary

6015

Woman Standing Alone

End of wide-forest road and start of single-track trail.

If the Autumn Creek Trail begins to descend. You have gone to far!

Barbed-wire tree on north side of trail.

× 5730

SCALE 1:12000

Route from Park boundary to Dancing Lady Summit.

National Geographic Trails Illustrated Maps
Glacier/Waterton Lakes National Parks, Two Medicine (315)
covers the approach to the route for Dancing Lady Mountain.

7) Respect Wildlife

ROUTE PROFILE

Elevations and distances are not exact due to variations in the chosen route.

Image provided by mytopo.com

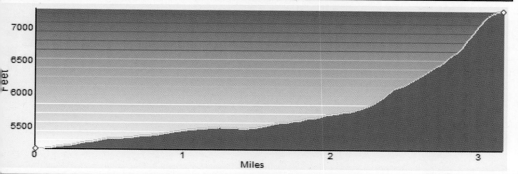

Total elevation change from Park Boundary to Dancing Lady summit is 2,260 feet (688 m) and the total distance is 3.25 miles (5.2 km).

GPS WAYPOINTS

GPS Waypoints are best used in conjunction with a compass, topo map, and common sense.

Relying solely on a GPS for navigation is NOT recommended.

	Latitude	Longitude	Elevation (ft/m)
Midvale Creek Trailhead (p. 21)	48.44247	-113.22188	4,803/1,464
UTM	12 0335 680E	53 67 647N	NAD27
ubec Lake Trailhead (p. 21)	48.37176	-113.27964	5,098/1,554
UTM	12 0331 216E	53 59 916N	NAD27
1] Park Boundary	48.37176	-113.27964	5,142/1,567
UTM	12 0332 997E	53 67 264N	NAD27
2] Begin Off-Trail Route	48.37176	-113.27964	5,729/1,746
UTM	12 0330 932E	53 65 864N	NAD27
3]Mid-point of Route	48.37176	-113.27964	6,571/1,743
UTM	12 0330 148E	53 66 210N	NAD27
4] Summit of Dancing Lady	48.37176	-113.27964	7,333/2,235
UTM	12 0329 827E	53 66 492N	NAD27

Panorama of the Continental Divide from Dancing Lady.

Photo from the Firebrand Pass Trail

UNIQUE VIEWS ON A CLASS II ROUTE WITH A HALF MILE (800 M) OF OFF-TRAIL TRAVEL.

Difficulty: Tolerable, due to trail mileage
GMS Climb Rating: Class (II) 3 MS
Time Required: 5-7 hours
Season: June to October
One-way Distance: 5.8 miles / 9.3 km
Elevation Change*: 2,783 ft / 848 m

Elevation: 7,891 feet / 2,405 m
Rank in Height: 175 of 234
Trailhead: Lubec Lake
U.S.G.S. Topo Map: Squaw Mountain
Trails Illustrated Map: Two Medicine 315
First Recorded Ascent: Unknown

* Elevation Change From Trailhead On Featured Route

Date Climbed: _____
Climbed With: _____
Notes: _____
_____
_____
_____
_____
_____

Red Crow Mountain is located along the Continental Divide near the southeastern boundary of Glacier National Park. There are a number of people for whom the peak could be named. Perhaps Red Crow Mountain was named for Red Crow, son of "Chief Black Bear" and nephew of "Seen From Afar." The name "Red Crow" is not associated with a bird that is red. The name describes what happens when sunshine reflects off a crow's feathers giving it a shining-reddish hue. This is powerful medicine to the Blackfeet since Napi makes this happen.

According to his great grandson, Jack Gladstone, Red Crow was born about 1830 and like his father was an influential leader of his people. Red Crow was a member of the "Fish Eaters" clan of the Kainai (*Blood tribe of the Blackfeet*). They were so named after resorting to breaking through the ice and catching bull trout to feed the people during a brutal winter in the 1840s. Eating fish was not respected by the Blackfeet whose diet consisted of red meat. The "Fish Eaters" were first mocked by other clans but they rose to prominence through leadership of Black Bear and Red Crow.

Red Crow became chief after his father died from smallpox. Jack Gladstone said, "After the Baker Massacre on January 23, 1870 Red Crow realized the futility of fighting the U.S. Army and sought to help his people transition from a nomadic Great Plains lifestyle of hunting buffalo to make peace with the federal governments." Red Crow encouraged the Canadian Mounted Police intervention in whiskey running after he saw the detrimental effects it had on his people. Red Crow also participated in crucial negotiations with the Canadian government to secure better lands for his people after Treaty 7 was ratified. Jack Gladstone is a modern-day singer and song writer who regales park visitors and others across the nation with stories and songs about his people.

There are two established routes for Red Crow Mountain. The recommended route leaves Firebrand Pass and follows the Continental Divide to the summit. Another less-traveled route traverses through the alpine area below Firebrand Pass to Lena Lake and then follows an animal trail to the Continental Divide and finally to the summit of Red Crow.

The *Lubec Lake Trailhead* (p. 21) is located at U.S. Highway 2 at mile marker #203 between East Glacier and Marias Pass. Look for the trailhead sign and follow the Coonsa Trail for 1.4 miles (2.2 km) to the Autumn Creek Trail Junction. From there follow the trail 1 mile (1.6 km) to the Firebrand Pass Junction. Follow the Firebrand Pass trail for 2.4 miles (3.8 km) to Firebrand Pass.

The Ole Creek Drainage from the route to Red Crow Mountain.

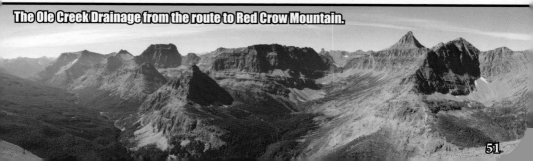

RED CROW MOUNTAIN

ROUTE INFORMATION

The route viewed from Calf Robe Mountain.

(1)

Rocky section of ridgeline. See photo on top of next page.

Long traverse along the ridge top.

Alternate route to ridge top.

Initial section that must be ascended from Firebrand Pass. There are numerous routes through this section! See photo below.

Firebrand Pass

CRUX

The route travels along the Continental Divide from Firebrand Pass. The views along the route are extremely rewarding!

A prominent goat/climbers trail climb across this scree slope. Climb up the slope and through the trees to reach the area behind this point.

It is possible to climb towards this point to access the ridge as well. This way requires more elevation gain.

Ascend through the loose scree to the more solid footing in the trees. Most climbers select one of the many goat trails that cross Firebrand Pass and climb to the ridge above the pass. There is a small bit of scrambling through rocks if desired on the west side of this ridge.

(A)

In photo: Kris Gross and Mike Gross

Follow the ridgeline to the area below this prominent point.

Follow the ridge from above Firebrand Pass to the cliffs shown in photo. This is not a difficult area to route find.

1

There are numerous goat trails ... find one and follow it!

In photo: Chris Rost

Climb above this point. The false summit is above this rocky section of the ridge.

Do your part to preserve the park. Don't remove anything from the park. See page 17

Climb around the set of the cliffs. Either side is safe.

This area is not difficult to negotiate and the false summit will soon be in sight.

There is nothing more than Class II climbing here unless a more challenging route is desired.

...rom the ...lse summit ...alk along ...e talus cov...red ridge to ...e summit.

Summit of Red Crow Mountain

1

View of Ole Creek Drainage.

A long-horned beetle. Photo by John VanArendonk.

Photo by John VanArendonk

1) Unsafe behavior in bear country

Return down the scree to the false summit and descend through the cliffs. Follow one of the many game trails that parallel the Continental Divide and return to Firebrand Pass.

If the snowbanks below Firebrand Pass are dangerous consider traversing above or below them from Firebrand Pass to the hiking trail.

Do a lot of "Heybearing" throughout this trip. Carry your bear spray. This is bear country!

Return to the *Lubec Lake Trailhead* (p. 21) via the Firebrand Pass Trail, the Autumn Creek Trail, and finally the Coonsa Trail.

This griz track was less than 1/4 mile from the Lubec Lake Trailhead.

RED CROW MOUNTAIN

OTHER OPTIONS

There are a few options for those who want to spend a bit more time poking around the area.

1) Continue to Two Medicine Valley along the Continental Divide on the "*Two Medicine Traverse*" (p. 58-59).

2) Climb **Calf Robe Mountain** (p. 34) from Firebrand Pass and descend from there via the Northeast Ridge Route to the Autumn Creek Trail.

3) It is possible for intermediate climbers with a lot of daylight left to traverse to **Dancing Lady Mountain** (p. 42) along the ridge from the pass north of Red Crow Mountain.

Do not attempt the route from Dancing Lady Mountain to Red Crow Mountain unless the group is proficient at cross-country travel on an unmarked route. It is crucial to have a topo map, compass, and GPS Waypoint of the trail access for the Autumn Creek Trail.

This wolf track was just a short distance from the Lubec Lake Trailhead.

SINCE 1910, THERE HAVE BEEN 10
DOCUMENTED DEATHS IN GLACIER
NATIONAL PARK DUE TO BEAR ATTACKS.

Summit, Little Dog, Elk, Sheep, Brave Dog, 8888, Barrier Buttes,

Eagle Ribs, Cloud Croft, Grizzly

Dancing Lady, Lena Lake, East Glacier

2) Failure to let family and/or friends know of your specific plans or route

RED CROW MOUNTAIN

ROUTE MAP

Legend:

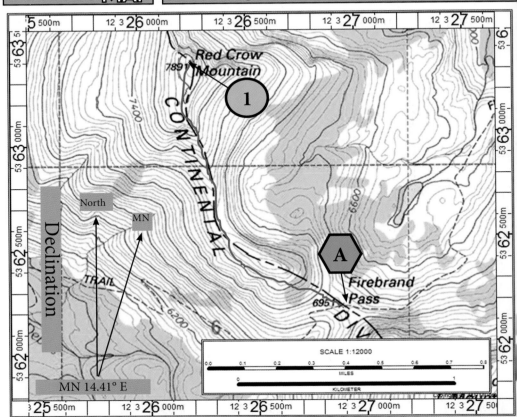

Your brain is the most important tool you take climbing ... use it!

National Geographic Trails Illustrated Maps
Glacier/Waterton Lakes National Parks, Two Medicine (315)
covers the approach to the route for Red Crow Mountain.

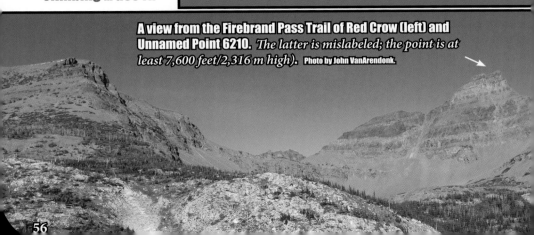

A view from the Firebrand Pass Trail of Red Crow (left) and Unnamed Point 6210. *The latter is mislabeled; the point is at least 7,600 feet/2,316 m high).* Photo by John VanArendonk.

Elevations and distances are not exact due to variations in the chosen route.

Image provided by mytopo.com

Total elevation change from Firebrand Pass to Red Crow Mountain summit is 1,086 feet (331 m) and the total distance is 1.0 miles (1.6 km).

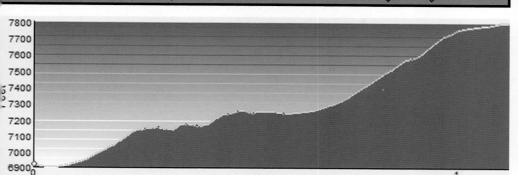

GPS Waypoints are best used in conjunction with a compass, topo map, and common sense.

Relying solely on a GPS for navigation is NOT recommended.

	Latitude	Longitude	Elevation (ft/m)
Lubec Lake Trailhead (p. 21)	48.37176	-113.27964	5,098/1,554
UTM	12 0331 216E	53 59 916N	NAD27
Autumn Creek Junction	48.37959	-113.30549	5,485/1,671
UTM	12 0329 286E	53 60 841N	NAD27
Firebrand Pass Trail Junction	48.39211	-113.30449	5,518/1,681
UTM	12 0329 402E	53 62 231N	NAD27
A) Firebrand Pass	48.39110	-113.33820	6,951/2,118
UTM	12 0326 903E	53 62 194N	NAD27
] Red Crow Mountain	48.40119	-113.34739	7,891/2,405
UTM	12 0326 257E	53 63 336N	NAD27

Lena Lake from near Red Crow Mountain, Photo by John VanArendonk.

This route travels between the Lubec Lake Trailhead (p. 21) and the Tw[o] Medicine Valley in Glacier National Park.

The route can be completed from either direction but is described here fron[m] Lubec Lake to the Two Medicine Valley. It will be necessary to leave a car a[t] the Scenic Point Trailhead (p. 20) or the Lubec Lake Trailhead.

The traverse passes through alpine country that offers phenomenal views o[f] the Continental Divide and a number of drainages. Although it would not b[e] necessary to summit any peaks along the route there are a number of option[s] for peak bagging as well.

The first portion of the route consists of climbing Red Crow Mountain (p. 50). The off-trail route begins at Firebrand Pass.

Firebrand Pass Trail

Continue on one of the many goat trails from Red Crow Mountain to the pas[s] below Bearhead Mountain (p. 60). This pass has unofficially been called "De[ ]Santo Pass" after Jerry DeSanto, a long-time Park Ranger. It may be fitting t[o] call this traverse the "DeSanto Pass Traverse." During this traverse Jack Stra[w] Lake is seen at the head of the Ole Creek Drainage. Buttercup Park can b[e] seen from the pass. In September there is a great chance of hearing elk bug[le] on this trip From "DeSanto Pass" two options area available.

Either traverse north to the saddle between Buttercup Park and Midvale Creek or climb up the scree field to the summit of Bearhead Mountain and then drop down to the saddle.

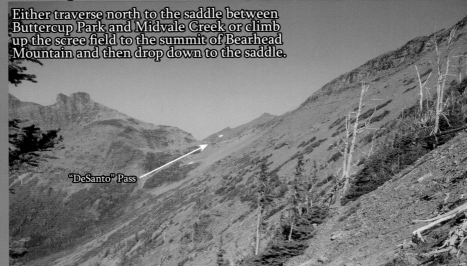

"DeSanto" Pass

Recommended route to Mount Ellsworth

If you are not summiting Ellsworth climb on goat trails to the ridge from the saddle.

The next objective is to climb to the scree slope below Mount Ellsworth (p. 68) from the saddle between Buttercup Park and Midvale Creek. A goat trail leads through the scree. If desired a short side trip to the summit of Mount Ellsworth adds just another 30-40 minutes to the trip.

From the ridge below Ellsworth traverse across the scree filled basin to Point 8650 and follow the goat trail to the north down to the Appistoki saddle.

Climb the ridge from the saddle to Point 8650.

Point 8650

Another short side trip up Appistoki Peak (p. 90) will add 40 to 50 minutes to the trip time.

From the Appistoki saddle drop down to the valley floor and follow the creek down toward the Mount Henry Trail.

The only difficult portion of this section is navigating around the high set of waterfalls that cannot be seen from above. There are numerous ways to get around them; stay on the east side, spend some time exploring, find a safe route for your group.

Switchback on Mount Henry Trail and exit from the Two Medicine Traverse.

Total Distance:
14 - 16 miles (22-25 km)

Total Elevation change:
6,000 to 7,000 feet
(1,828 - 2,133 m) depending on route.

Trip time between 8-12 hours.

It may be best to wait until later in the season to attempt this route if there is a great amount of snow. There are potentially dangerous conditions if snow is on the route.

Bearhead Mountain

REFERENCE SECTION

FIREBRAND TO DESANTO PASS ROUTE
and
NORTHERN APPROACH ROUTE

Photo taken from Mount Ellsworth route.

A SELDOM CLIMBED PEAK ON THE CONTINENTAL DIVIDE

Difficulty: Challenging
GMS Climb Rating: Class II (3) LL
Time Required: 8 - 10 hours
Season: Late June to October
One-way Distance: See Route Section
Elevation Change*: See Route Section

Elevation: 8,406 feet / 2,562 m
Rank in Height: 132 of 234
Trailhead: Lubec Lake
U.S.G.S. Topo Map: Squaw Mountain
Trails Illustrated Map: Two Medicine 315
First Recorded Ascent: Unknown

* Elevation Change From Trailhead On Featured Route

Date Climbed: _____
Climbed With: _____
Notes: _____
_____
_____
_____
_____
_____

Bearhead Mountain sits on the Continental Divide above unofficially named "DeSanto Pass" and a saddle between seldom-visited Buttercup Park and the Midvale Creek Basin. It is hard to say how many visitors actually reach this isolated peak each year. Certainly very few climbers set out with a goal to make their final destination the summit of Bearhead Mountain. It is more of a place to stop while en route to other destinations that are perhaps deemed more worthwhile.

Those who have climbed to the summit have most likely been completing the traverse from Firebrand Pass to the Two Medicine Valley. The route passes through DeSanto Pass below the summit. This book refers to that traverse as the *"Firebrand Pass to Two Medicine Traverse"* (p. 58-59).

DeSanto Pass.

Bearhead Mountain seems like a lonely point on the map that perhaps deserves a bit more recognition from climbers. Although it isn't a "major" peak in the park, it is still a worthwhile destination for any climber who sets out to reach its summit. Take some time and get there!

It requires a long day to reach Bearhead from either the south by way of **Red Crow Mountain** (p. 50) or from the north by following the **Mount Ellsworth** (p. 68) route. Both have their advantages and disadvantages.

The "sign" for DeSanto Pass.

Firebrand Pass has a longer and higher approach via trail but has greater elevation gain. Goat trails traverse the entire length of the Continental Divide from Firebrand to DeSanto Pass.

Approaches from the north can be made from either the *Scenic Point Trailhead* (p. 20) via Mount Ellsworth or from the *South Shore Trailhead* (p. 20) via **Never Laughs Mountain** (p. 98). Prepare for major elevation gains and losses either way!

ROUTE INFORMATION

GMS Climb Rating: Class II (3) LL
One-way trail distance: 4.8 miles (7.7 km)
One-way off-trail distance: 3.5 miles (5.6 km)
Elevation gain: 5,946 feet (1,812 m)
Elevation loss: 2,710 feet (826 m)

From **Red Crow Mountain** (p. 50): Follow a goat trail north from Red Crow Mountain to the next saddle.

Walk to DeSanto Pass is not an official name but it is a fitting name to honor long-time park ranger Jerry DeSanto.

Traverse as viewed from goat trail north of Red Crow Mountain.

2

"DeSanto Pass"

Beginning of goat trail.

Saddle

1

Jackstraw Lake is just out of view in this photo.

A marvelous goat trail traverses on the southwest slope above Jackstraw Lake to "DeSanto Pass."

CRUX

Blue bar indicates same feature in both photos.

From DeSanto Pass clim[b] 906 feet (276 m) throug[h] the scree slopes and class I[I-] III cliffs to the summit.

It is possible, but certainl[y] less enjoyable, to avoid all [of] the cliffs on this ascent. Th[e] scree is loose and the soli[d] footing near the cliffs make[s] it easier to ascend.

The summit is located just above this large clump of cliffs. Climb around on either side or climb through the crack in the cliff wall. There is another short section of scree below the summit.

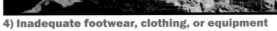

4) Inadequate footwear, clothing, or equipment

NORTHERN APPROACH ROUTE:

GMS Climb Rating: Class II (3) LL
One-way trail distance: 1.5 miles (2.4 km)
One-way off-trail distance: 7 miles (11.2 km)
Elevation gain: 5,210 feet (1,588 m)
Elevation loss: 2,064 feet (629 m)

Follow the **Mount Ellsworth** (p. 68) route.

Rather than climbing to the summit of Ellsworth drop down to the saddle between Bearhead and Ellsworth. From there it is necessary to climb through the scree slope to the summit cairn.

This view shows a route from the ridge below Mount Ellsworth to the summit ridge of Bearhead.

Walk down the scree slope to the saddle between Paradise Park and Midvale Creek. Locate and follow one of the many goat trails that climb to the summit ridge. The upper goat trail is more traveled and therefore easier to follow.

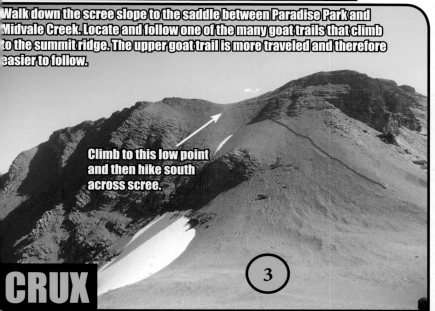

Climb to this low point and then hike south across scree.

CRUX

3

From the saddle hike south through Class II scree field to the summit cairn.

4

Dancing Lady Mountain is seen behind the false summit.

This photo is of the false summit. The views are good from there if you want to check them out!

Do your part to preserve the park. Don't destroy existing cairns. See page 17

BEARHEAD
MOUNTAIN

RETURN
ROUTE

Returning from Bearhead Mountain presents an interesting conundrum. *Is it easier to retrace the route to the starting trailhead or choose an alternate ending?* Much of that depends upon weather conditions and the length of time remaining in the day. It also depends where you have left a vehicle or vehicles.

If the climb began at the *Scenic Point Trailhead* (p. 20) it is just a little further to retrace the route to **Mount Ellsworth** (p. 68) and then summit **Never Laughs Mountain** (p. 98) before returning to the *South Shore Trailhead* (p. 20).

It is also a great trip to complete the *Firebrand Pass to Two Medicine Traverse* (p. 58-59) between *Lubec Lake Trailhead* (p. 21) and the Two Medicine Valley in either direction.

BEARHEAD
MOUNTAIN

OTHER
OPTIONS

1) If using the Northern Approach from the *Scenic Point Trailhead* consider summiting either **Mount Henry** (p. 78) or **Appistoki Peak** (p. 90).

2) Another option is to hike to **Scenic Point** (p. 88), this may be rather anticlimactic after hitting the summits on the way to Bearhead Mountain.

3) If the day includes the *Firebrand Pass to Two Medicine Traverse* consider climbing **Calf Robe Mountain** (p. 34) from Firebrand Pass.

4) It is also possible to drop down to Lena Lake from the saddle between **Red Crow Mountain** (p. 50) and Bearhead. There is a bit of route finding and bushwhacking from the outlet of the lake to the Firebrand Pass Trail. As a navigation aid aim for the northern ridge of Calf Robe where it reaches the Firebrand Pass Trail (*see photo below*).

There is less brush on the east side of Lena Lake. Follow the shore line to the outlet and then make a bushwhack to the Firebrand Pass Trail.

Aim for any portion of the peak to the right of the yellow line.

Location of the outlet of Lena Lake and the upper headwater of Railroad Creek.

SUMMIT VIEWS

BETWEEN 1913 AND 1995 ... 46 PEOPLE DIED BY DROWNING IN THE PARK, 27 BY HEART ATTACKS, AND 26 BY VEHICLE ACCIDENTS.

Red Crow, Summit, Little Dog, Elk, Sheep, Brave Dog, 8888, Grizzly

Rockwell, Stimson, Flinsch, Sinopah, Ellsworth, Rising Wolf, Henry

Mount Saint Nicholas makes a cameo appearance through the September wildfire-produced haze while the Continental Divide continues its path on a agged ridgeline between Bearhead and Grizzly.

6) Lack of skill or fitness level for type of terrain or outing

U.S.G.S. Map: Squaw Mountain, MT
Contour Interval = 40 feet

Image provided by mytopo.com
Map Produced by the U.S. Geological Service

Northern Approach Route
Map shows route from Ellsworth

Firebrand Pass to DeSanto Pass Route
Map shows route from North of Red Crow

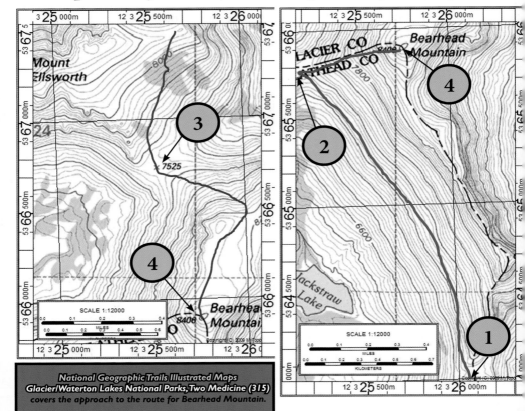

National Geographic Trails Illustrated Maps
Glacier/Waterton Lakes National Parks, Two Medicine (315)
covers the approach to the route for Bearhead Mountain.

A climber approaches the summit.
In photo: Micah Tinkham

Take a kid on a fun climb and inspire the next generation to learn to love the high country.

Take a friend climbing and make some memories!

ROUTE PROFILE

Elevations and distances are not exact due to variations in the chosen route.

Image provided by mytopo.com

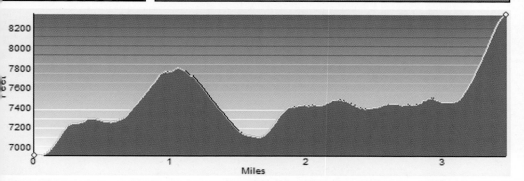

Total elevation change from Firebrand Pass to Bearhead Mountain is 3,400 feet (1,036 m) and the total distance is 3.75 miles (6 km).

BEARHEAD MOUNTAIN

GPS WAYPOINTS

GPS Waypoints are best used in conjunction with a compass, topo map, and common sense.

Relying solely on a GPS for navigation is NOT recommended.

	Latitude	Longitude	Elevation (ft/m)
Lubec Lake Trailhead (p. 21)	48.37176	-113.27964	5,098/1,554
UTM	12 0331 216E	53 59 916N	NAD27
Scenic Point Trailhead (p. 20)	48.48516	-113.36040	5,202/1,585
UTM	12 0325 582E	53 72 698N	NAD27
1] Red Crow - Bearhead Saddle	48.40747	-113.34997	7,111/2,167
UTM	12 0326 088E	53 64 040N	NAD27
2] DeSanto Pass	48.42310	-113.36319	7,446/2,296
UTM	12 0325 163E	53 65 807N	NAD27
3] Bearhead - Ellsworth Saddle	48.43152	-113.35867	7,525/2,293
UTM	12 0325 526E	53 66 733N	NAD27
4] Summit	48.42424	-113.35506	8,406/2,562
UTM	12 0325 768E	53 65 915N	NAD27

Bearhead Mountain from Dancing Lady Mountain.

7) Impaired or poor judgment due to physical problems

Photo taken from Bearhead Mountain.

AN EXTENDED RIDGE WALK IN OPEN COUNTRY TO A LONELY SUMMIT WITH COMMANDING VIEWS

Difficulty: Challenging
GMS Climb Rating: Class II(3) LM
Time Required: 8 - 10 hours
Season: Late June to October
One Way Distance: 6.1 miles/ 9.8 km
Elevation Change*: 3,379 feet / 1,029 m

* Elevation Change From Trailhead On Featured Route

Elevation: 8,581 feet / 2,615.5 m
Rank in Height: 110 of 234
Trailhead Location: Scenic Point
U.S.G.S. Topo Maps: Squaw Mountain and Mount Rockwell
Trails Illustrated Map: Two Medicine 315
First Recorded Ascent: Unknown

Date Climbed: _____
Climbed With: _____
Notes: _____
_____
_____
_____
_____
_____

Mount Ellsworth may be named for an early Glacier National Park packer named Billy Ellsworth. At least that is what the original park surveyor R. T. ~ans said. That's all that is known about this mystery man. It R. T. Evans should know; he was there when it all began.

would be fun to think that Glacier's Mount Ellsworth could be linked to Antarctica's ~ount Ellsworth which rises 9,596 feet (2,924 m) above sea level. The one in Antarctica rtainly is named for Lincoln Ellsworth. His first claim to fame was in 1926 when he ~rticipated in the Norwegian explorer Roald Amundsen's 2nd Aerial Expedition to the ~rth Pole. They spotted the North Pole on May 12, 1926. This was the first undisputed ~hting of the North Pole. Ellsworth visited Glacier after this significant event.

~ncoln Ellsworth also made four aerial expeditions of Antarctica. One of those flights ~s Trans-Antarctic from Dundee Island to the Ross Ice Shelf. His record-making flight ~vered 2,200 miles (3,540 km) in about 20 hours. During these flights Ellsworth claimed ~er 300,000 acres of the huge continent for the United States.

~ncoln Ellsworth is also tied to the naming of the Sentinel and Heritage Ranges which ~ake up the Ellsworth Mountains. The total land area of the Ellsworth Mountains is 200 ~iles (360 km) long and 30 miles (48 km) wide. Vinson Massif at 16,050 feet (4,892 m) in ~e Heritage Range is the highest peak on the continent of Antarctica.

~hat we know for sure is that George Schultz said that this mountain was called "*Buffalo ~ild*" or "*Inokos*" in honor of a Blackfeet warrior.

~OUNT ~LLSWORTH

TRAILHEAD ~NFORMATION

The *Scenic Point Trailhead* (p. 20) is located on the south side of the Two Medicine Road just before arriving at the Two Medicine Campground and Store. Parking is adequate and the trail takes off on the east side of the gravel parking lot. The trail is called the <u>Mount Henry Trail</u>.

~e trail is easy to follow and within a short distance is a spur trail leading to the right the <u>Appistoki Falls Overlook</u>. *Unless you have a lot of time in the day you can skip see-~ this because the waterfalls up the drainage on the climbing route are as impressive.* Stay

the left and work through ~e woods on the north-~st side of Appistoki Creek ~rough a series of switch-~cks. Eventually, Appistoki ~eek will be far below and ~e trail heads southeast ~ about ½ mile. Soon the ~que below **Mount Henry** ~78) opens up and a sharp ~itchback turning north ~ reached. It is from this ~itchback that the off -trail ~rtion of the route begins.

Photo of Rockwell, Painted Tepee, Never Laughs, Sinopah, Flinsch, and Aster Valley from the route.

MOUNT ELLSWORTH

ROUTE INFORMATION

Mount Henry

Point 8650

Photo taken from the Mount Henry Trail.

There are many routes to the top of the waterfalls. The red lines show two possible routes.

The switchback on Mount Henry Trail

After leaving the trail at the switchback traverse to the upper waterfall. Try to maintain as much elevation as possible since it will ALL need to be regained

It is also possible to drop down and follow Appistoki Creek to the upper waterfall and then into the valley underneath Mount Henry. See Photo below

Appistoki saddle

U.S.G.S. Point 8650

Eventually the elevation lost will need to be regained plus quite a bit more to the saddle to the south of Appistoki Peak. A side trip to the twin summits of **Appistoki Peak** (p. 90) will take an additional 40-50 minutes round trip from this saddle.

Upper waterfall

Photo taken from saddle below Medicine

Mount Ellsworth

It is also possible to summit Mount Ellsworth from Mount Henry. Traverse from the summit of Henry to Point 8650 and join the route as described in above photos.

← Climb up the ridge to Point 8650

← Grizzly Mountain

Mount Ellsworth

Never Laughs Mountain

Photo from the Appistoki route.

From Appistoki Saddle climb up a goat/climbers' trail to Point 8650.

Avoid the temptation to traverse ACROSS the slope. This ends in sketchy cliffs and would require gaining the ridge to complete the route.

From the unnamed peak (U.S.G.S. Point 8650) a goat trail leads to the next point. Descend into the saddle between that point and Mount Ellsworth. It is another mile or so to the summit of Ellsworth.

2

3

1

U.S.G.S. Point 8650

U.S.G.S. Point 8650

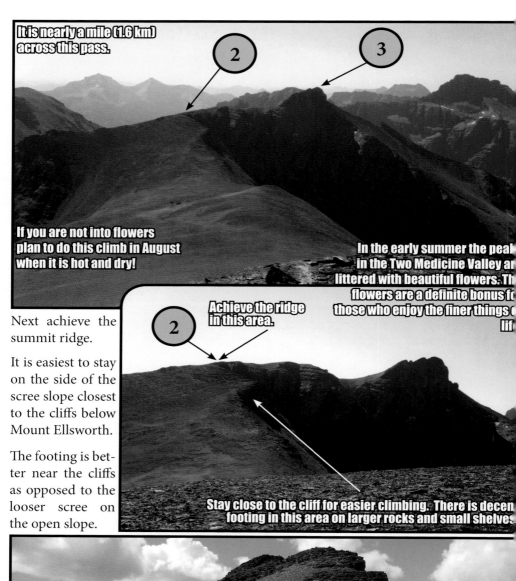

It is nearly a mile (1.6 km) across this pass.

2

3

If you are not into flowers plan to do this climb in August when it is hot and dry!

In the early summer the peak in the Two Medicine Valley ar littered with beautiful flowers. Th flowers are a definite bonus fo those who enjoy the finer things o lif

Next achieve the summit ridge.

It is easiest to stay on the side of the scree slope closest to the cliffs below Mount Ellsworth.

The footing is better near the cliffs as opposed to the looser scree on the open slope.

Achieve the ridge in this area.

2

Stay close to the cliff for easier climbing. There is decen footing in this area on larger rocks and small shelves

There is little difficulty on the rest of the route.

Route finding as well as navigation to Mount Ellsworth is uncomplicated as the summit is clearly visible for a large portion of the ascent.

2

Climb through the scree towards the cliffs on the ridgeline. There is a nice goat climber trail traveling through the scree

72

A closer view of the scree field and cliff band.

photos: Becky Neumann, Isaiah Neumann, and Chris Rost

Summit cairn with PVC pipe register is located behind this point.

3

Do your part to preserve the park. Don't build new cairns or wind blocks. See page 17

Class III climbing through the cliffs surrounding the summit is enjoyable. There are many ways to reach the summit.

MOUNT ELLSWORTH

RETURN ROUTE

MOUNT ELLSWORTH

Appistoki Peak   U.S.G.S. Point 8650   Mount Henry

1

Retrace your route to 8650 and cruise down to the Appistoki saddle. Summit Appistoki Peak (p. 90) and add another one to your Glacier Summits list.

MOUNT ELLSWORTH

OTHER OPTIONS

1) It is not difficult to summit **Mount Henry** (p. 78) fro Point 8650. Loop around the south side of 8650 and follow t goat trail eastward to the summit. This side trip will take abo 45 minutes if you walk slowly. It will be necessary to gain son elevation as well as work around the small points on the rid but a decent goat/human trail follows the ridge for the enti distance until the final push to the summit. It may be best to save this for the return rou

It is possible to continue to **Medicine** (p. 89) and the Mount Henry Trail from Mou Henry. The only tricky part here is getting off Henry's summit dome. This is not difficu after down climbing through the first set of cliffs just south of the summit dome. Wo down to the right then left through the scree filled slopes for around 250 feet of elevatio loss and then follow the climber's trail to the ridge between Mount Henry and Medicin Intermediate climbers may be interested in crossing the arête below Mount Henry.

2) **For intermediate climbers with good route finding skills!** Continue down the northwe slope of Mount Ellsworth to **Never Laughs Mountain** (p. 98) and summit it. Follow t return route descriptions found on the Never Laughs Mountain section.

3) A long walk along a goat trail to the south and west along the Continental Divide w eventually lead to Firebrand Pass. From Firebrand Pass follow the hiking trail to event ally arrive the *Lubec Lake Trailhead* (p. 21) on U.S. Highway 2 east of Marias Pass.

4) It is also possible to summit Ellsworth from **Never Laughs Mountain** (p. 98). Th route is straightforward after reaching the summit of Never Laughs. For more details the approach see "*A Traverse In Reverse*" on page 101.

SUMMIT VIEWS

THE LEWIS AND CLARK EXPEDITION CAME WITHIN 50 MILES OF THE PRESENT DAY PARK BOUNDARY WHEN THEY TRAVELED ALONG THE MARIAS RIVER IN 1806.

A panorama from the summit of Mount Ellsworth.

Bearhead, Red Crow, Calf Robe, Summit, Little Dog, 8888, Grizzly

Grizzly, St. Nicholas, Rockwell, Stimson, Flinsch, Morgan

Never Laughs, Rising Wolf, Spot, Appistoki, Point 8650, Henry

Take a moment to read trailhead signs. They contain important information.

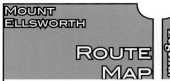

MOUNT
ELLSWORTH

ROUTE
MAP

Legend:

U.S.G.S. Map: Squaw Mountain, MT
Contour Interval = 40 feet

Image provided by mytopo.com
Map Produced by the U.S. Geological Service

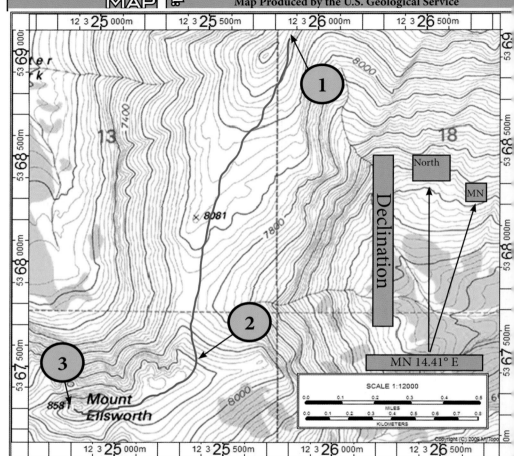

National Geographic Trails Illustrated Maps
Glacier/Waterton Lakes National Parks, Two Medicine (315)
covers the approach to the route for Mount Ellsworth.

Another nice view from the Ellsworth route.

**Elevations and distances are not exact
due to variations in the chosen route.**

Image provided by mytopo.com

The off-trail portion of route from the Mount Henry Trail to summit of Mount
Ellsworth has a total off-trail distance of 4.5 miles (7.2 km) and an off-trail elevation
gain of 3,341 feet (1,018 m) and an elevation loss of 1,222 ft (372 m).

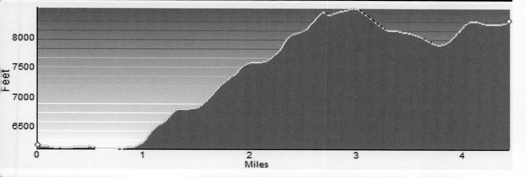

**GPS Waypoints are best used in conjunction with
a compass, topo map, and common sense.**

**Relying solely on a GPS for navigation
is NOT recommended.**

	Latitude	Longitude	Elevation (ft/m)
Scenic Point Trailhead (p. 20)	48.48516	-113.36040	5,202/1,585
UTM	12 0325 582E	53 72 698N	NAD27
Off-trail Begins At Switchback	48.47582	-113.33980	6,230/1,898
UTM	12 0327 066E	53 71 614N	NAD27
Appistoki Creek Crossing	48.46034	-113.34488	6,801/2,072
UTM	12 0326 644E	53 69 905N	NAD27
Appistoki Saddle	48.46141	-113.35547	7,667/2,336
UTM	12 0325 865E	53 70 048N	NAD27
1] Point 8650	48.45382	-113.35431	8,650/2,636
UTM	12 0325 925E	53 69 202N	NAD27
2] Ellsworth Ridge	48.43784	-113.36165	8,330/2,538
UTM	12 0325 327E	53 67 442N	NAD27
3] Mount Ellsworth	48.43625	-113.36918	8,581/2,615
UTM	12 0326 903E	53 62 194N	NAD27

Bearhead Mountain and "DeSanto" Pass from the Ellsworth route.

Mount Henry

SCENIC POINT ROUTE

Photo taken near Point 8650

THE HIGH POINT OF A CLASSIC RIDGE-TOP TRAVERSE

Difficulty: Challenging
GMS Climb Rating: Class II (3) MM or II (4) MM depending on chosen route
Time Required: 6-10 hours
Season: Mid-June to October
One-way Distance: 5 miles / 8 km
Elevation Change*: 3,645 feet / 1,111 m

Elevation: 8,847 feet / 2,696.5 m
Rank in Height: 76 of 234
Trailhead: Scenic Point
U.S.G.S. Topo Map: Squaw Mountain
Trails Illustrated Map: Two Medicine 315
First Recorded Ascent: Unknown

* Elevation Change From Trailhead On Featured Route

Date Climbed: _____
Climbed With: _____
Notes: _____
_____
_____
_____
_____
_____
_____

The Two Medicine Valley played an important role in the early days of Glacier National Park. It served as an important hub for the trail rides that the Great Northern Railroad used to promote tourism in the park in their "*See America First*" promotion. Tourists would come from across the United States and spend their days riding horseback from one area of the

park to another. Great Northern Railroad also built Swiss-style chalets for its guests. Sadly, the Two Medicine Lodge was burned after World War II due to being in disrepair. One of the Railroad's plans to promote tourism was to place bells on summits across the park, as is done in Europe, in hopes that bells could be heard ringing across the park. According to park history, there was a large bell on the Mount Henry Trail but it and all of the other bells were scrapped as steel to help with the war effort during World War II.

A Glacier flower garden

Mount Henry is part of a thirteen mile route called the "Scenic Point Ridge Walk." This amazing route crosses three named Glacier Park peaks including Medicine, Mount Henry, and Appistoki Peak. If timed right much of the route will have brilliant flowers springing out of the scree. The route also passes through an area where the resident bighorn sheep band likes to hang out. This route provides an enjoyable day with incredible views into the Nyack and Two Medicine Valleys.

In spite of having an elevation of 8,847 feet, Mount Henry is not one of Glacier's well known peaks. Due to its location on the eastern side of the park Mount Henry can be climbed earlier than many others and it is a good warm up climb for the season.

From the *Scenic Point Trailhead* (p. 20) walk through trees until the spur junction to the Appistoki Falls Overlook. Follow the main trail through a series of switchbacks. After breaking out of the trees, Appistoki Creek can be seen far below the trail. At the western-most switchback a portion of Henry's north face can be seen. This is the point that must be reached after descending from Appistoki. Continue on the trail through a series of switchbacks to the highest point of the trail before reaching Scenic Point. Walk across the portion of the trail that is flat to the eastern side of the ridge and leave the trail there. A large cairn on the north side of the trail marks a good place to start traversing.

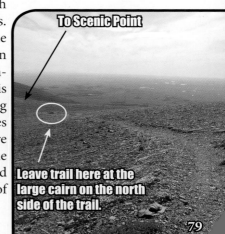

To Scenic Point

Leave trail here at the large cairn on the north side of the trail.

Early morning starts are recommended.

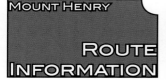

ROUTE INFORMATION

Leave the Mount Henry Trail **AFTER** crossing the flat section of the trail (7,400 feet/2,255 m)below Scenic Point (once Lower Two Medicine Lake can be seen from the trail).

From here walk on the east side of ridge to the next saddle.

Mount Henry was called Wolf Calf by the Native Americans.

Medicine

Mount Henry

1

There are many routes to the summit ridge.

The route through this area is much less important than the destination.

The Head and Bison Mountain

An elevation gain of a little over 1,000 feet (304 m) is needed to reach the summit Of Medicine from the saddle.

Climb through a mixture of vegetation, scree and talus to the ridge. There is less scree on the northeast side of the slope toward the saddle with Bison Mountain.

Once on the ridge walk southwest to the cairn on Medicine.

The final slope of Mount Henry is shown.

The arête on Mount Henry

2

Photo by John VanArendonk

Cairn on Medicine

Continue up this splendid ridgeline from Medicine until an arête blocks easy access to the summit of Mount Henry's east ridge.

It is not necessary to climb to the top of every point along the ridge. Goat trails occasionally lead the climbers along the ridgeline.

Consider distance, elevation, weight carried, physical condition

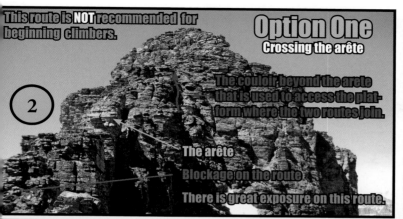

This route is **NOT** recommended for beginning climbers.

2

Option One
Crossing the arête

The couloir beyond the arête that is used to access the platform where the two routes join.

The arête

Blockage on the route

There is great exposure on this route.

At this **blockage** there are **Two Options** to reach a platform that transitions to an easy class 3 scramble to the actual summit.

Confident climbers can cross the arête and scramble to the summit through a **couloir**.

CRUX

Option One is **NOT** recommended for beginning climbers.

Climb on the left (SOUTH) side of the arête.

This climber is standing on the other side of the large table-sized rock.

The maneuver to the break between the near and middle climbers is seen in this photo. This may be the most difficult section of the climb. Take your time and search for a mid-way foot hold to safely reach this point.

In photo: GMS members

At the end of the arête climb to the top of a large table-sized rock and then descend to where the climber is standing. Climb the couloir in photo below. See page 84 for a photo from above the arête.

Work across the arête by scrambling around the small pillars that form the top of the arête. This is Class IV due to a fall surely resulting in serious injury or death. Stay on the south side of the arête.

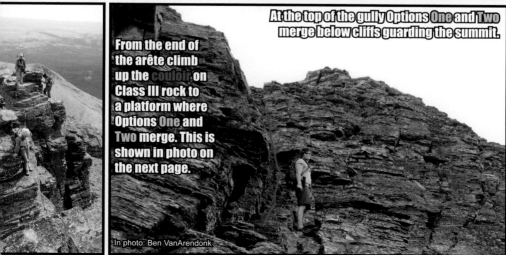

From the end of the arête climb up the couloir on Class III rock to a platform where Options One and Two merge. This is shown in photo on the next page.

At the top of the gully Options One and Two merge below cliffs guarding the summit.

In photo: Ben VanArendonk

eather, and hours of daylight remaining.

CRUX

Option Two
Southeast Gully

There may be snow in the gully. Carefully climb above or below the snow to reach the other side.

From the blockage at the arête drop down to the left (southwest) and follow a goat trail. After passing below the lowest set of cliffs as seen from the arête continue along the trail to a lower finger of rocks. Once past this lower finger locate a scree-filled gully that can be climbed.

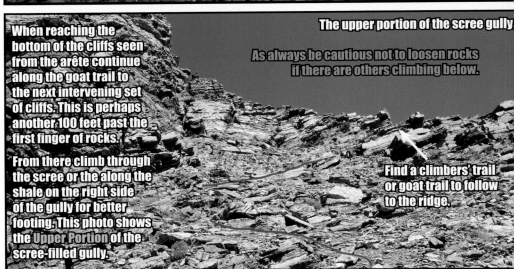

The upper portion of the scree gully

As always be cautious not to loosen rocks if there are others climbing below.

When reaching the bottom of the cliffs seen from the arête continue along the goat trail to the next intervening set of cliffs. This is perhaps another 100 feet past the first finger of rocks.

From there climb through the scree or the along the shale on the right side of the gully for better footing. This photo shows the Upper Portion of the scree-filled gully.

Find a climbers' trail or goat trail to follow to the ridge.

From the platform where the routes merge climb through Class II and III cliffs to the summit.

In photo: Brooks Baer

There are a few way through the cliffs below the cairn.

Enjoy the views an continue traversin to the southwest t Point 8650.

If no further climb ing is desired th route can be retrace with little difficul or continue to **Apistoki Peak (p. 90)**

Snow covers some trails well into July, so be prepared to do some route finding.

RETURN ROUTE

It is possible to retrace the entire route back to the *Scenic Point Trailhead* (p. 20) but why would one want to do that when there are more peaks to explore?

If exploring more of the park is on the agenda see **Other Options** and the **Route Information** sections for guidance on additional routes. **Remember it is always further than you think it is, it is always higher than you think it is, and it always takes more time than you think it should!**

Point 8650

Follow the trail off Mount Henry to Point 8650 which is seen at the end of the RED line. From Point 8650 complete the Scenic Point Traverse by descending to the Appistoki Saddle or continue to Mount Ellsworth (p. 68) to extend the trip.

In photo: Read Vaughan, Andy Engdahl and Tim Anderson

Follow a goat trail to the Appistoki Saddle. Climb Appistoki Peak if desired!

Appistoki saddle

From the saddle drop into the Appistoki Creek Drainage and return to the southern-most switchback on the Mount Henry trail as described in the Trailhead Section (p.79) section of this route.

Do your part to preserve the park. Don't alter existing structures such as cairns. See page 17

Set a pace that all party members can handle.

Three options are present for extending the day from Mount Henry. Choose accordingly depending on time remaining for the trip.

1) Summit **Appistoki Peak** (p. 90) from the Appistoki saddle by ascending 500 feet (152 m) to the summit. Follow descent instruction located in the Appistoki Peak section of this guidebook.

2) Retrace the route to Mount Henry Trail and return to trailhead. This needs no further explanation!

3) Continue to **Mount Ellsworth** (p. 68) and other peaks such as **Bearhead Mountain** (p. 60) or **Never Laughs Mountain** (p. 98).

The Mount Henry Arete Route

Photo by Franz Barthel.

In photo: GMS Members

Medicine

Looking back along the arête on Mount Henry.

Always stay on the south side of the arête until reaching this large table-like slab. Climb to the top of the slab and then descend either the south or north side to reach the couloir.

2

The maneuver to the break before the large table-like rock in the arête may be the most dangerous part of this section of the climb. Take your time and search for a mid-way foot hold to safely reach this point.

A view from the route between Medicine and Henry.

SUMMIT VIEWS

EACH FRESH PEAK ASCENDED TEACHES SOMETHING. — SIR MARTIN CONWAY

Ellsworth, Grizzly, Sheep, St. Nicholas, Vigil, Battlement, Rockwell

Summit, Little Dog, Bearhead, Elk, Mount Despair, Sheep, Point 8888

U.S.G.S. Map: Squaw Mountain, MT
Contour Interval = 40 feet

Image provided by mytopo.com
Map Produced by the U.S. Geological Service

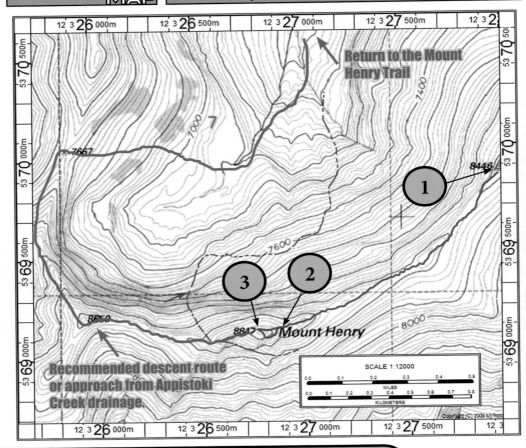

Return to the Mount Henry Trail

1

2

3

Mount Henry

Recommended descent route or approach from Appistoki Creek drainage.

SCALE 1:12000

MILES

KILOMETERS

Copyright (C) 2009 MyTopo

The summit and north face of Mount Henry.

The arête below Mount Henry.

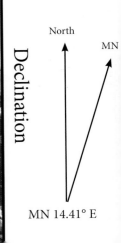

North

MN

Declination

MN 14.41° E

ROUTE PROFILE

Elevations and distances are not exact due to variations in the chosen route.

Image provided by mytopo.com

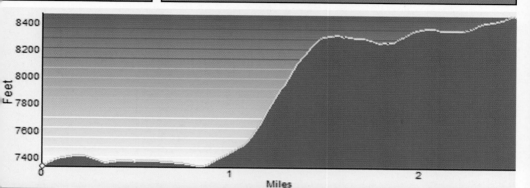

Total off-trail elevation change from Mount Henry Trail to Mount Henry is 2.75 miles (4.4 km) and the route gains 1,528 feet (465 m).

MOUNT HENRY

GPS WAYPOINTS

GPS Waypoints are best used in conjunction with a compass, topo map, and common sense.

Relying solely on a GPS for navigation is NOT recommended.

	Latitude	Longitude	Elevation (ft/m)
Scenic Point Trailhead (p. 20)	48.48516	-113.36040	5,202/1,585
UTM	12 0325 582E	53 72 698N	NAD27
Henry Off-Trail Route	48.48028	-113.32628	7,400/2,255
UTM	12 0328 086E	53 72 079N	NAD27
1] Medicine Peak	48.46036	-113.32706	8,446/1,585
UTM	12 0327 962E	53 69 867N	NAD27
2] Arête	48.45338	-113.34061	8,665/2,641
UTM	12 0326 936E	53 69 121N	NAD27
3] Summit	48.45315	-113.34256	8,847/2,696
UTM	12 0326 791E	53 69 100N	NAD27

National Geographic Trails Illustrated Maps Glacier/Waterton Lakes National Parks, Two Medicine (315) covers the approach for Mount Henry.

Bighorn sheep along the route.

Scenic Point

A hiking trail leads all the way to Scenic Point. This challenging on-trail hike is 3.1 miles (5 km) in distance and gains 2,240 feet (682 m) in elevation from the Scenic Point Trailhead (p. 20).

The first 2.25 miles (3.6 km) climbs in earnest after a generally flat trail to the Appistoki Falls Overlook allows a bit of a warm up. At that spur trail continue up the trail through switchbacks that make the climb longer but easier than climbing straight up the slope.

Eventually the trail reaches a saddle and the remainder of the trail is generally flat. Follow the trail to the next junction sign and then take the left fork up the slope to Scenic Point.

Please stay on the trail at all times!

In photo: Read Vaughan

Views From The Route

Scenic Point

Follow the Mount Henry Trail to the flat area below Scenic Point as shown in the photo on page 81 of the Mount Henry route page.

In this meadow traverse west to the saddle below Medicine (See Mount Henry p. 78 for details). Climb through Medicine's scree field to the summit ridge. Hike southwest along the ridge until the summit cairn is reached on the far end.

The next portion entails retracing the route along the summit ridge and then dropping down to Bison Mountain. The scree may be loose in places so be cautious during the descents.

Cross the plant covered slope to the summit of Bison Mountain and then descend down the slope to The Head.

To return traverse below the scree slope of Medicine back to the saddle below Medicine and then return to the Mount Henry Trail.

It only takes another 15 - 20 minutes to hike to Scenic Point on the trail. Return to the Scenic Point Trailhead.

Total One-Way Distance: 7.0 miles/11.3 km

Total Elevation Gain: 4,487 feet/1,367 m

Route Rating: Class 2 (III)

Route Views

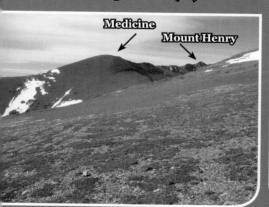

Do your part to preserve the park. Don't prospect for minerals. See page 17

89

Appistoki Peak

APPISTOKI CREEK ROUTE

Photo taken at North Shore Trailhead

Class II & III Climbing With Commanding Views Of Two Medicine Valley

Difficulty: Tolerable, due to trail mileage
GMS Climb Rating: Class II(3) MS
Time Required: 5-8 hours
Season: Mid-June to October
One-way Distance: 4.6 miles / 7.4 km
Elevation Change*: 2,962 feet / 902 m

Elevation: 8,164 feet / 2,488 m
Rank in Height: 158 of 234
Trailhead: Scenic Point
U.S.G.S. Topo Map: Squaw Mountain
Trails Illustrated Map: Two Medicine 315
First Recorded Ascent: Unknown

* Elevation Change From Trailhead On Featured Route

Date Climbed: _____
Climbed With: _____
Notes: _____
_____
_____
_____
_____
_____

Appistoki Peak, an unassuming peak with two summits, stands above the southeast shore of Two Medicine Lake. The route to this 8,164 foot (2,488 m) peak passes through the Appistoki Creek Valley. Climbers who attempt this peak at the right time of the year will pass through meadows of wild flowers while Appistoki Creek cascades over waterfalls in the bottom of the valley. Keep your eyes open for bighorn sheep in this area as well.

Appistoki Peak was named by R. T. Evans, a topographer who worked on mapping the park. According to the park records,

"Looking over" the Two Medicine Valley from Appistoki Peak.

Evans inquired from his Native American guide what word the Blackfeet used for "looking over something," and the guide, misunderstanding the meaning of his question responded "*Appistoki*," for the Blackfeet spirit who looks over everything and everyone.

The name "*appistoki*" appears to be appropriate for this peak as it truly does look over a lot of territory. Views from Appistoki Peak offer a unique perspective on the Two Medicine Valley, the plains of Central Montana, and into the Nyack region as well.

Enjoy the walk through the trees from the *Scenic Point Trailhead* (p. 20). A short side-trip on a spur trail rewards hikers with a beautiful view of <u>Appistoki Falls</u>. Continue up the trail on the numerous switchbacks.

After breaking out of the trees the trail climbs through a series of switchbacks until reaching a large southeastern-most switchback that yields views of part of Mount Henry's north face.

Remember any elevation lost traversing to the waterfalls will need to be regained.

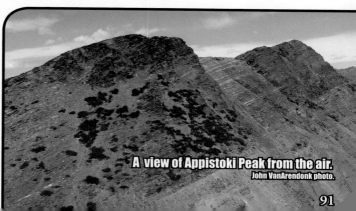

A view of Appistoki Peak from the air.
John VanArendonk photo.

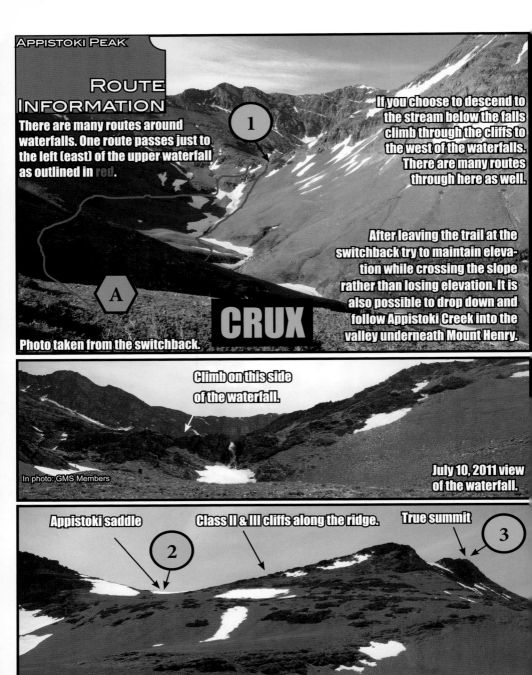

APPISTOKI PEAK

ROUTE INFORMATION

There are many routes around waterfalls. One route passes just to the left (east) of the upper waterfall as outlined in red.

If you choose to descend to the stream below the falls climb through the cliffs to the west of the waterfalls. There are many routes through here as well.

After leaving the trail at the switchback try to maintain elevation while crossing the slope rather than losing elevation. It is also possible to drop down and follow Appistoki Creek into the valley underneath Mount Henry.

CRUX

A

Photo taken from the switchback.

Climb on this side of the waterfall.

In photo: GMS Members

July 10, 2011 view of the waterfall.

Appistoki saddle

Class II & III cliffs along the ridge.

True summit

2

3

See page 70 for additional photos of the route.
View of ridge from the route.

Photo from above waterfalls.

From the top of the second waterfall climb up the solid scree and vegetated slope to the saddle south of Appistoki Peak. Find the best way for your group. It is also possible to climb up the slope to the ridge below the peak. There are Class III cliffs guarding the ridgeline but it is possible to climb through them.

OTHER IMPORTANT POINTS TO REMEMBER:

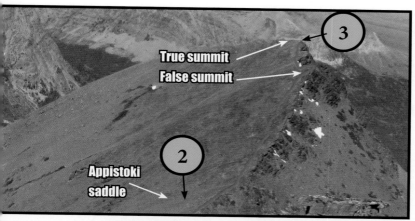

True summit

False summit

3

2

Appistoki saddle

A Class II trail leads up the ridge from the Appistoki saddle towards the twin summits of the peak.

The large red slabs are loose in places so watch the footing.

Carefully work below the ridge on a route that is best for your climbing ability.

"Carefully" is used to warn about rolling an ankle.

The climb is about 800 feet from the saddle to the twin summits.

A view of the route from the Appistoki saddle to the false summit.

A climber's trail can be followed from Appistoki saddle to the false summit.

There is a slight loss of elevation from the false summit (southern) to the true summit which is the northern point. It does not take much time to stand on both.

Appistoki Peak's summit cairn.

Do your part to preserve the park. Don't gather firewood unless allowed. See page 17

RETURN ROUTE

Descend from Appistoki Peak by choosing one of the two options outlined below. Each route will return to the switchback on the Mount henry Trail and end at Scenic Point Trailhead.

Pasqueflower on the route.

1) Return to the Appistoki saddle and retrace the route to the switchback.

2) **This option is for intermediate to advanced climbers.** Climbers with good route-finding skill can descend on the north side of the true summit of Appistoki Peak to a ramp that slopes east to the 6,000 feet contour level and return to the trail near the switchback via a wide scree-filled gully *(see photo below).*

OTHER OPTIONS

This climb is unique because in and of itself it can be a spectacular climb for beginning climbers. It can also be combined with the other peaks to make a full day for mountaineers with intermediate to advanced skills.

A view of Appistoki Peak from the Mount Henry Trail in July 2011.

1) Include it as the last peak in the Scenic Point Ridge Walk or the *Firebrand Pass to Two Medicine Traverse* (p. 58-59).

2) Summit Appistoki prior to climbing **Mount Ellsworth** (p. 68) and/or **Never Laughs Mountain** (p. 98).

3) Return to the Appistoki saddle and climb the ridge to Point 8650 and then return via the route of ascent.

1916 - BROWNING, MONTANA:
THE TEMPERATURE DROPPED FROM PLUS
46° F. TO MINUS 56° F IN 24 HOURS.
A 100° F CHANGE IN A SINGLE DAY!

Sinopah, Phillips, Helen, Stimson, Flinsch, Rising Wolf

Never Laughs, St. Nicholas, Painted Tepee, Rockwell, Sinopah

The park service closes trails for a reason ... do not go past a trail closure sign.

Legend:

U.S.G.S. Map: Squaw Mountain, MT
Contour Interval = 40 feet

Image provided by mytopo.com
Map Produced by the U.S. Geological Service

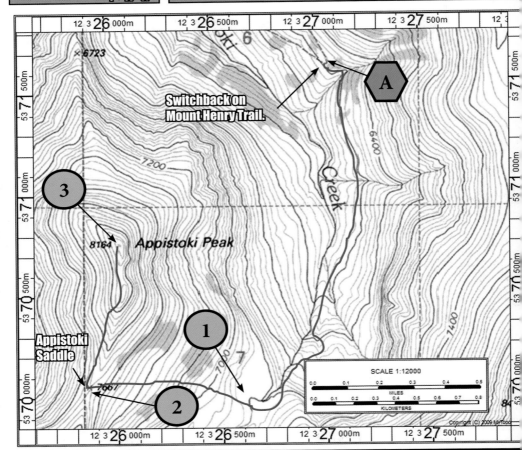

Switchback on
Mount Henry Trail.

A

Appistoki Peak

Appistoki
Saddle

SCALE 1:12000

National Geographic Trails Illustrated Maps
Glacier/Waterton Lakes National Parks, Two Medicine (315)
covers the approach to the route for Appistoki Peak.

A view to the south from Appistoki Peak.

ROUTE PROFILE

Elevations and distances are not exact due to variations in the chosen route.

Image provided by mytopo.com

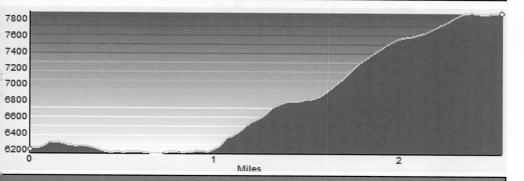

Off-trail statistics from Mount Henry Trail to Appistoki Peak :
2.62 miles (4.2 km) and gains 2,172 feet (662 m).

GPS WAYPOINTS

GPS Waypoints are best used in conjunction with a compass, topo map, and common sense.

Relying solely on a GPS for navigation is NOT recommended.

		Latitude	Longitude	Elevation (ft/m)
Scenic Point Trailhead (p. 20)		48.48516	-113.36040	5,202/1,585
	UTM	12 0325 582E	53 72 698N	NAD27
A) Off-trail Begins At Switchback		48.47582	-113.33980	6,230/1,898
	UTM	12 0327 066E	53 71 614N	NAD27
] Appistoki Creek Crossing		48.46034	-113.34488	6,801/2,072
	UTM	12 0326 644E	53 69 905N	NAD27
] Appistoki Saddle		48.46141	-113.35547	7,667/2,336
	UTM	12 0325 865E	53 70 048N	NAD27
] Appistoki Summit		48.46771	-113.35350	8,164/2,448
	UTM	12 0325 925E	53 69 202N	NAD27

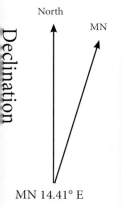

North

MN

Declination

MN 14.41° E

Approaching the Appistoki Saddle from Point 8650 in July 2011.

BUTTERCUP PARK TRAIL ROUTE

Never Laughs from the air with Ellsworth and Grizzly in background, John VanArendonk photo

FEEL THE JOY OF STANDING ON THE SHORTEST PEAK IN THE TWO MEDICINE VALLEY; IT WILL CURE WHAT AILS YOU!

Difficulty: Tolerable, due to trail mileage
GMS Climb Rating: Class III(3) MS
Time Required: 5-8 hours
Season: July to October
One-way Distance: 3.75 miles / 6 km
Elevation Change*: 2,510 feet / 765 m

Elevation: 7,641 feet / 2,329 m
Rank in Height: 189 of 234
Trailhead: South Shore
U.S.G.S. Topo Map: Mount Rockwell
Trails Illustrated Map: Two Medicine 31
First Recorded Ascent: Unknown

* Elevation Change From Trailhead On Featured Route

Date Climbed: _____
Climbed With: _____
Notes: _____
_____
_____
_____
_____
_____

Never Laughs Mountain is found along the southern shore of Two Medicine Lake in the Two Medicine Valley of Montana's Glacier National Park. This particular Two Medicine Lake is actually the middle lake of three lakes that are all named Two Medicine Lake. Lower Two Medicine Lake lies to the northeast and part of its waters are within the park boundary while the remainder is contained in the Blackfeet Indian Reservation. Upper Two Medicine Lake is tucked away between Sinopah Mountain and Mount Helen. Never Laughs is reached by an enjoyable walk away from the *North Shore Trailhead*. Never Laughs is flanked by the Aster Creek Drainage to the east and the Paradise Creek Drainage to the west.

The summit of Never Laughs Mountain is low for Glacier National Park standards at just 7,641 feet (2,329 m) in elevation and the true summit is just one of a number of points along a ridge that runs above the southern shore of the middle of the Two Medicine Lakes to Mount Ellsworth. **Never Laughs is historic Blackfeet family name.**

All of the named neighboring peaks on the south side of Two Medicine Lake overshadow Never Laughs Mountain. Even points with no name are higher such as the unnamed point that is 8,650 feet (2,636 m) high along the ridge between Henry and Appistoki.

"Saintgrizzly" referred to Never Laughs Mountain as **"terminally depressed."** It is easy to appreciate his humorous reference and also understand why this mountain is in need of some serious psychotherapy. The conclusive diagnosis for Never Laughs Mountain would be chronic little-peak syndrome resulting from an overwhelming inferiority complex and pervasive low self-esteem due to lack of elevation compared to its peers … perhaps this explains why it "**NEVER LAUGHS!**"

For the **FINAL** and **MOST DEMEANING** insult, Never Laughs stands 9 feet (3 m) shorter than Painted Tepee Peak. There is little joy for a mountain that isn't even taller than a painted tepee.

From the *South Shore Trailhead* (p. 20) enjoy a walk through trees for 2.25 miles (3.6 km) to the junction of the abandoned Buttercup Park Trail which has not been maintained for years.

The trail may be difficult to find but if you cross the suspension bridge over Paradise Creek you have missed it!

The trail is generally easy to follow, but there are short sections of trail that disappear in thick vegetation for 15 to 20 feet (5-6 m) Walk beyond the overgrown area and it will be located again. Make lots of noise by "heybearing" while traveling on this abandoned trail!

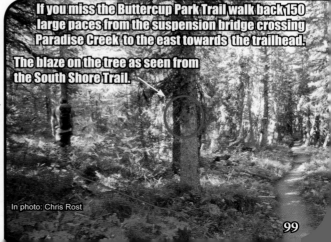

If you miss the Buttercup Park Trail walk back 150 large paces from the suspension bridge crossing Paradise Creek to the east towards the trailhead.

The blaze on the tree as seen from the South Shore Trail.

In photo: Chris Rost

99

NEVER LAUGHS MOUNTAIN

ROUTE INFORMATION

See GPS Waypoints for a recommended place to leave this trail.

Follow the Buttercu Park Trail for about mile (1.6 km). Lea the trail and gain a proximately 1,200 fe (365 m) through t brush and scree un below the cliffs.

It is a good idea have a GPS with th route waypoints loa ed prior to climbir this route. The fore is thick in places.

Climb through the open-forested, northern slope of Never Laughs towards the summit ridge. Find places to climb through the cliff bands that are safe for your group.

It is also possible to traverse another .5 mile (.8 km) to the south along a bench and climb through the numerous breaks in the cliffs to the saddle between Never Laughs and Ellsworth.

The area below the north saddle. There are many ways to reach the summit ridge. CRUX

See GPS Waypoints for recommended ascent routes!

There are a number of oj tions to achieve the ridg Once on the ridge, walk t the summit of Never Laugh and feel the joy. There is high-point on the norther end of the ridge but the tru summit is marked with summit cairn (see photo on t of the next page).

Scree on the route.

Do not travel across areas that are closed for restoration.

The false summit from Never Laughs summit.

The north saddle.

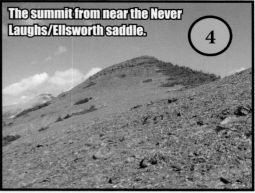

The summit from near the Never Laughs/Ellsworth saddle.

4

Bonus Route: A Traverse In Reverse

3 2 1

Reach the Mount Ellsworth - Never Laughs saddle.

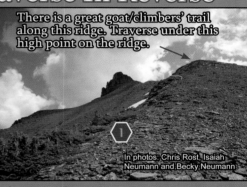

There is a great goat/climbers' trail along this ridge. Traverse under this high point on the ridge.

1

In photos: Chris Rost, Isaiah Neumann and Becky Neumann

2

The goat trail traverses below the high point on the ridge.

This is truly an epic way to see a lot of the Two Medicine Valley in one day. The route covers approximately 12 miles and has around 4,500 to 5,000 feet in elevation gain and loss.

Follow the suggested route to Never Laughs Mountain (p. 98). From the summit of Never Laughs ascend the west ridge of Mount Ellsworth (p. 68) follow the reverse route to Mount Henry (p. 78) or Appistoki Peak (p. 90) and then to the Scenic Point Trailhead (p. 20).

Follow the ridge to the summit block. There are many places to climb through the cliffs on the south side of the block.

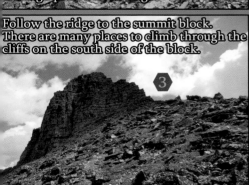

3

The easier route is from the southeast corner of the summit block.

NEVER LAUGHS MOUNTAIN

RETURN ROUTE

Buttercup Park Trail Descent Route: ——————

If this descent is considered traverse to the lowest saddle t the north of the true summit. Descend beside a scree-filled gully for about 1,000 feet to a large scree field. Work along t the right while descending through the scree fields. Eventually it will be necessary to drop down into the lush valley floor and bushwhack until yo (hopefully) locate the old Buttercup Park Trail. It is easy to miss this trail in the thic underbrush and downfalls. This trail will lead to the South Shore Trail and then back t the *South Shore Trailhead* (p. 20) at Two Medicine.

Use the provided GPS Waypoint [1] on page 105 to help locate the old trail!

Aster Park Descent Route: ══════════

This route was recommended by Dr. J. Gordon Edwards in "*A Climber's Guide to Glacie National Park.*" This is a logical route for descent but expect some difficulties here as wel There are a number of places to descend off the true summit. Skirt below the cliffs on th Never Laughs side of the drainage. Eventually (*hopefully*) you will join in with the Aste Falls Trail and follow it to the South Shore Trail and then back to the Two Medicine Park ing Lot. *The writers have not used this route.*

A Traverse In Reverse: ══════════

It is possible to climb from Never Laughs to **Mount Ellsworth** (p. 68) and reverse th route from Point 8650 to either **Mount Henry** (p. 78)/**Medicine** (p. 89) or even **Appistok Peak** (p. 90).

The goal is to reach the Mount Henry Trail near Scenic Point by summiting Mount Henr or at the western switchback if summiting Appistoki Peak. Once at the *Scenic Point Trail head* (p. 20) walk the short distance to the Two Medicine Parking lot and the *South Shor Trailhead*. **See page 101 for more details.**

NEVER LAUGHS MOUNTAIN

OTHER OPTIONS

A staggering amount of options are included in the multipl ways to reach this peak.

All of the peaks accessed from *Scenic Point Trailhead* (p. 20 could be included in a day climb with Never Laughs Moun tain. It just depends upon how far you want to go and hov hard you are willing to work.

1) Since Never Laughs Mountain in and of itself is not a full day for many climbers, con sider hiking to Aster Falls on the return trip.

2) Consider a longer hike to Rockwell Falls which is located on the Two Medicine Pas Trail. See **Sinopah Mountain** (p. 132) for details on how to reach Rockwell Falls.

3) Walk all the way around Two Medicine Lake. Once back at the South Shore Trail wal over the suspension bridge and take the right fork at the Two Medicine Pass Trail. Onc at the inlet end of the lake the trail flattens out and swings along the northern side of th lake to the *North Shore Trailhead* (p. 20). Walk to the Two Medicine Parking lot and th *South Shore Trailhead* (p. 20). Total trail distance is 7.4 miles (11.9 km).

THERE ARE MANY PATHS TO THE TOP OF THE MOUNTAIN, BUT THE VIEW IS ALWAYS THE SAME. - CHINESE PROVERB

Grizzly, Two Medicine Pass, Chief Lodgepole, Painted Tepee, Rockwell

Sinopah, Rising Wolf

Spot, Two Medicine Lake, Appistoki, Point 8650

Yield right of way to hikers passing from behind or traveling uphill.

U.S.G.S. Map: Mount Rockwell
Contour Interval = 80 feet

Image provided by mytopo.com
Map Produced by the U.S. Geological Service

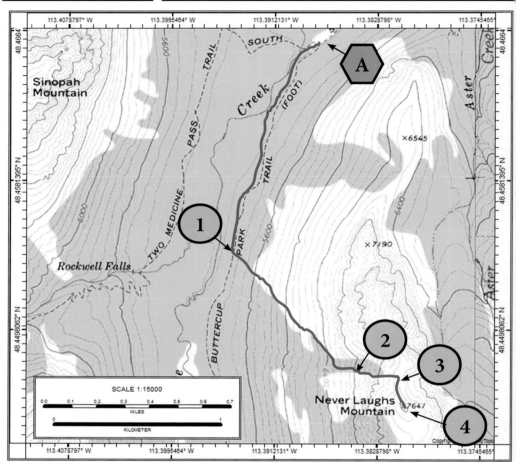

National Geographic Trails Illustrated Maps
Glacier/Waterton Lakes National Parks, Two Medicine (315)
covers the approach to the route for Never Laughs Mountain.

The northeast ridge of Never Laughs
from the North Shore Trailhead (p. 20).

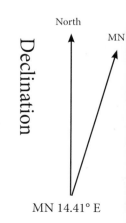

North

MN

Declination

MN 14.41° E

Elevations and distances are not exact due to variations in the chosen route.

Image provided by mytopo.com

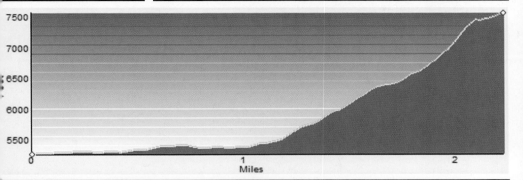

Statistics for Off-Trail Route from South Shore Trail to Never Laughs Mountain: 2,701 feet (823 m) and the total distance is 2.4 miles (3.9 km).

GPS Waypoints are best used in conjunction with a compass, topo map, and common sense.

Relying solely on a GPS for navigation is NOT recommended.

	Latitude	Longitude	Elevation (ft/m)
South Shore Trailhead (p. 20)	48.48313	-113.36822	5,170/1,583
UTM	12 0335 680E	53 67 647N	NAD27
A) Start Buttercup Park Trail	48.46557	-113.38759	5,267/1,605
UTM	12 0323 528E	53 70 606N	NAD27
1] Leave Buttercup Park Trail	48.45363	-113.39470	5,406/1,647
UTM	12 0322 938E	53 69 273N	NAD27
2]Climb Through Cliffs	48.44780	-113.38463	6,800/2,072
UTM	12 0323 662E	53 68 601N	NAD27
3] Northern Saddle	48.44881	-113.36149	7,368/2,245
UTM	12 0323 898E	53 68 707N	NAD27
4] Never Laughs summit	48.44559	-113.38082	7,641/2,329
UTM	12 0323 936E	53 68 348N	NAD27

Never Laughs from the Sinopah Mountain Route.

Painted Tepee Peak

TWO MEDICINE PASS ROUTE

Photo taken from Chief Lodgepole Peak

A UNIQUE PEAK WITH INTERESTING VIEWS

Difficulty: Tolerable to Challenging
GMS Climb Rating: Class III (4) LS
Time Required: 6-8 hours
Season: Late June to October
One-way Distance: 8.5 miles / 13.6 km
Elevation Change*: 2,519 feet / 767 m

Elevation: 7,650 feet / 2,331.5 m
Rank in Height: 188 of 234
Trailhead: South Shore
U.S.G.S. Topo Map: Mount Rockwell
Trails Illustrated Map: Two Medicine 315
First Recorded Ascent: Unknown

* Elevation Change From Trailhead On Featured Route

Date Climbed: _____

Climbed With: _____

Notes: _____
_____
_____
_____
_____
_____

It is not difficult to see why this beautiful peak was named

Painted Tepee Peak all those years ago. The slopes are flooded with different shades of red, brown, green, and black. When viewed from the South Shore Trail the peak indeed does look like a Tepee (well sort-of if you use your imagination).

Painted Tepee Peak has an additional bonus of summiting Chief Lodgepole Peak on the climb. Its close proximity makes it a realistic yet challenging climb for those with the stamina to hike the Two Medicine Pass Trail to Chief Lodgepole Peak.

Perhaps the most outstanding feature of this diminutive peak is the perspective it offers on the taller peaks that surround it. There are actually 360° views from this summit.

Painted Tepee is located above the Paradise Creek Drainage. In the early years of the park the Buttercup Park Trail traveled up Paradise Creek and was used to access Two Medicine Pass. Although the Buttercup Park Trail can still be located it is in poor condition due to not being maintained for a number of years. Buttercup Park is a seldom-visited area tucked in behind Mount Ellsworth below unofficially named "DeSanto Pass." This area is truly wild. If you are in this area in September listen for elk bugling in Buttercup Park and the Paradise Creek Drainage during the "rut."

The only peak Painted Tepee "towers" over is Never Laughs Mountain, which is 8 feet (2.4 m) shorter than Painted Tepee Peak.

A wall of cliffs can be seen from Mount Rockwell all the way to Sinopah Mountain. Further northeast Rising Wolf dominates the scene, which eventually gives way to Spot Mountain, the Two Medicine Lakes, Appistoki Peak extends up to Mount Henry. Mount Ellsworth rises behind Never Laughs Mountain and the beautiful Paradise Park and Paradise Drainage lie below the imposing northeast face of Grizzly Mountain.

Painted Tepee from Sinopah Mountain

Follow the trail from the *South Shore Trailhead* (p. 20) to Two Medicine Pass. Do not be distracted by the numerous spur trails - stay on the main trail until reaching the Two Medicine Pass Trail. Follow the trail past Cobalt Lake and then up to the long ridge leading to **Chief Lodgepole Peak** (p. 126). The Two Medicine Pass Trail leads to Chief Lodgepole Peak's summit cairn.

Total trail distance is 7.5 miles (12 km) with an elevation gain of over 2,518 feet (767 m) due to numerous ups-and-downs on the route. The standard climbing route for Painted Tepee departs from Chief Lodgepole Peak.

Hikers need to yield to horses.

ROUTE INFORMATION

A series of gendarmes (rock spires) can be bypassed by traversing on the southeast side of the ridge. It is possible to climb over some of the pinnacles as well.

The summit

3

Route description written by John VanArendonk.

Make sure you are wearing a climbing helmet while climbing along the ridge.

In photos: Rod Graham and Mike VanArendonk

Photo by John VanArendonk

From the summit of Chief Lodgepole, look to the east and see Painted Tepee at the end of the ridge (*see photo page 106*).

Work east along this ridge heading towards the series of gendarmes at the end of the ridge.

It is easiest to approach along the south (right) side of the gendarmes.

Stay at the base of these cliffs following occasional goat trails. Continue walking east for approximately ½ mile (0.8 km) from the saddle.

The route to the summit is found near the "**balanced rock.**"

Total distance from Chief Lodgepole to Painted Tepee is about 1 mile (1.6 km).

The "balanced rock"

The "balanced rock"

Cross streams only where the trail intersects.

Just before reaching the **"balanced rock"**, follow a narrow ramp to the saddle between the balanced rock and summit ridge. Carefully pick your way up onto this narrow ridge and traverse back to the west and the eventual summit.

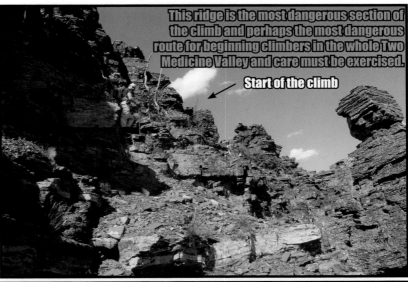

This ridge is the most dangerous section of the climb and perhaps the most dangerous route for beginning climbers in the whole Two Medicine Valley and care must be exercised.

Start of the climb

We recommend accessing the summit ONLY from this ridge.

It is almost like walking a balance beam.

A fall off this 50 ft. cliff could be fatal. In high winds this ridge would be extremely difficult with little room for error.

CRUX

After negotiating this ridge by whatever route seems passable, you gain the summit. Some stay on the very top of the ridge and walk, others crawl, still others drop down slightly to the left (southeast side) and traverse a little lower.

Retrace the route off the summit.

Photo by John VanArendonk.

Whatever method you choose to make this crossing, be very careful.

PAINTED TEPEE PEAK

RETURN ROUTE

Do not attempt to climb down the slope towards the Two Medicine Pass Trail or Cobalt Lake without the proper equipment, training, and experience.

There are numerous unseen and dangerous cliffs between the summit and the trail.

Cobalt Lake from near Chief Lodgepole Peak. Two Medicine Lake can be seen in the distance.

PAINTED TEPEE PEAK

OTHER OPTIONS

Painted Tepee Peak is often climbed with **Grizzly Mountain** (p. 114). Summit Grizzly first and then hit Painted Tepee.

Climbing other peaks on the same day is probably not realistic for all but the most fit climbers.

Instead consider:

1) Spend some time on the shore of Cobalt Lake before heading back to the trailhead. *It might be helpful to have insect repellent while sitting beside the shoreline.*

2) Stop at Rockwell Falls and explore the numerous pools and cascades that are found above the trail. Information on how to locate Rockwell Falls can be found in the **Sinopah Mountain** (p. 132) route section.

3) Follow a spur trail 0.1 miles (160 m) to Aster Falls and 0.7 miles (1.1 km) to the trail's end at Aster Park. The spur junction is 1.2 miles (1.9 km) from the *South Shore Trailhead* (p. 20).

MORE "LEAVE NO TRACE" IDEAS TO REMEMBER:

SUMMIT VIEWS

I HAVE CLIMBED SEVERAL HIGHER MOUNTAINS WITHOUT GUIDE OR PATH, AND HAVE FOUND, AS MIGHT BE EXPECTED, THAT IT TAKES ONLY MORE TIME AND PATIENCE COMMONLY THAN TO TRAVEL THE SMOOTHEST HIGHWAY. - HENRY DAVID THOREAU

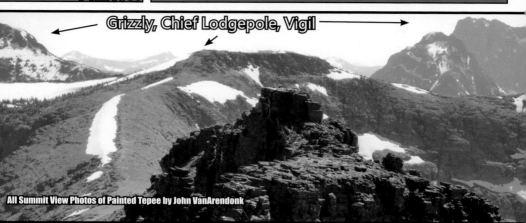

Grizzly, Chief Lodgepole, Vigil

All Summit View Photos of Painted Tepee by John VanArendonk

Grizzly, Despair, Eagle Ribs

Rising Wolf, Spot, Appistoki

Deer, goats, porcupines, and other animals are attracted by sweat and urine.

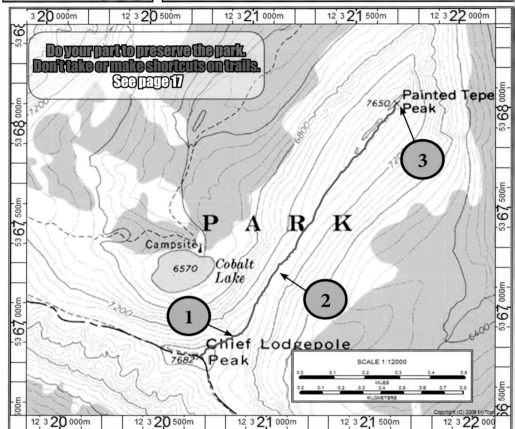

PAINTED TEPEE PEAK

ROUTE MAP

Legend:

U.S.G.S. Map: Mount Rockwell
Contour Interval = 80 feet

Image provided by mytopo.com
Map Produced by the U.S. Geological Service

Do your part to preserve the park.
Don't take or make shortcuts on trails.
See page 17

7650 × Painted Tepee Peak

3

P A R K

Campsite

6570   Cobalt Lake

2

1

Chief Lodgepole Peak

7682

SCALE 1:12000

0.0   0.1   0.2   0.3   0.4   0.5
MILES

0.0   0.1   0.2   0.3   0.4   0.5   0.6   0.7   0.8
KILOMETERS

Copyright (C) 2009 MyTopo

Something big and furry did this!

Carry bear spray and do a lot of "heybearing" on the routes!

Wear a climbing helmet any time there is a chance of rock fall!

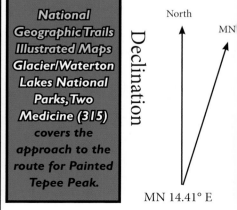

National Geographic Trails Illustrated Maps Glacier/Waterton Lakes National Parks, Two Medicine (315) covers the approach to the route for Painted Tepee Peak.

Declination

North

MN

MN 14.41° E

ROUTE PROFILE

Elevations and distances are not exact due to variations in the chosen route.

Image provided by mytopo.com

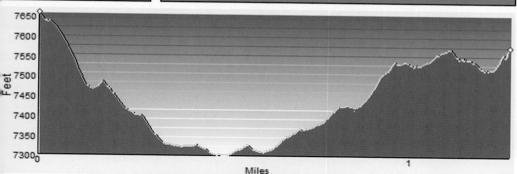

Total distance from Chief Lodgepole Peak to Painted Tepee Peak is 1.3 miles (2 km). The route gains 624 feet (190 m) and looses 706 feet (215 m).

GPS WAYPOINTS

GPS Waypoints are best used in conjunction with a compass, topo map, and common sense.

Relying solely on a GPS for navigation is NOT recommended.

	Latitude	Longitude	Elevation (ft/m)
South Shore Trailhead (p. 20)	48.48313	-113.36822	5,170/1,583
UTM	12 0335 680E	53 67 647N	NAD27
Two Medicine Pass junction	48.46578	-113.38770	5,384/1,641
UTM	12 0335 680E	53 67 647N	NAD27
Rockwell Falls	48.45315	-113.40204	5,439/1,658
UTM	12 0335 680E	53 67 245N	NAD27
Cobalt Lake	48.43476	-113.42460	6,570/2,002
UTM	12 0320 661E	53 67 647N	NAD27
Chief Lodgepole	48.43070	-113.42399	7,682/2,341
UTM	12 0320 692E	53 66 792N	NAD27
1] Climbers' Trail	48.43151	-113.42194	7,483/2,280
UTM	12 0320 847E	53 66 877N	NAD27
2] Mid-Point Of Ridge	48.43648	-113.41707	7,325/2,232
UTM	12 0321 224E	53 67 419N	NAD27
3] Summit	48.44227	-113.41120	7,650/2,331
UTM	12 0321 679E	53 68 049N	NAD27

The jagged ridge of Painted Tepee Peak from the Two Medicine Pass Trail.

Grizzly Mountian

TWO MEDICINE PASS ROUTE

Photo taken from Chief Lodgepole Peak

A SUBLIME CLIMB IN GLACIER NATIONAL PARK'S ALPINE WONDERLAND

Difficulty: Challenging, due to most mileage being gain on trails.
GMS Climb Rating: Class II (3) LM
Time Required: 8-12 hours
Season: July to October
One-way Distance: 9.3 miles / 15 km
Elevation Change*: 3,936 feet / 1,199 m

Elevation: 9,067 feet / 2,763.5 m
Rank in Height: 55 of 234
Trailhead: South Shore
U.S.G.S. Topo Map: Mount Rockwell
Trails Illustrated Map: Two Medicine 31?
First Recorded Ascent: Unknown

* Elevation Change From Trailhead On Featured Route

Date Climbed: _____
Climbed With: _____
Notes: _____
_____
_____
_____
_____
_____
_____

"Saintgrizzly" wrote...

Montana's entry in the seemingly omnipresent name-a-mountain-after-the-great-bear sweepstakes is Grizzly Mountain (the original Kootenai name was Big Grizzly Mountain). The state has only one so named, although there is a Grizzly Peak in the Custer National Forest (not far from Red Lodge); also, GNP does have one other peak making use of the word "grizzly"—Medicine Grizzly Peak, in the Cut Bank Area of the park. Grizzly Mountain is located in the park's Two Medicine area, is reached via a good trail, and even though it is necessary to leave that trail for the final almost mile-and-a-half ascent, is by no means a difficult climb. It is a true scramble, with the only drawback being that of length—9.5 miles from trailhead to summit—but that happenstance becomes secondary to the rewards, which, simply put, is that the trek winds through mountain wilderness at its best and after approximately eight miles, upon reaching Two Medicine Pass the views become...spectacular.

Grizzly Mountain reminds us of the Glacier's well-known grizzlies. They can be intimidating when met on the trail. The only things that makes this "grizzly" intimidating are the distances that must be traveled to reach its summit and the frequent-intense wind gusts that buffet hikers crossing the ridge between Mount Rockwell and Two Medicine Pass. Winds have been measured up to 80 mph in this area of the park and this particular pass is quite infamous for strong wind. If the wind is growling like a grizzly, it may be best to reschedule this climb and find a more sheltered climb.

In the early 1900s, the Great Northern Railway was promoting rail travel by encouraging Americans to "*See America First.*" To encourage tourism a number of Swiss-style chalets where constructed in Glacier National Park. The Two Medicine Lake Lodge served this area and tourists were taken by horseback on the trails. The Buttercup Park Trail which followed Paradise Creek was used during that era to access Two Medicine Pass. A direct climbing route was used from that trail to reach the summit of Grizzly Mountain. That trail can be found but is in poor shape or has totally disappeared due to years of neglect. It would be a challenge to climb Grizzly Mountain via this abandoned trail.

The Two Medicine Pass Route presents no significant challenges for climbers who are comfortable hiking up Class II scree and scrambling on Class III terrain. It is frequently climbed on the same day with Chief Lodgepole Peak and Painted Tepee Peak. This makes a lot of sense since all of these peaks are accessed from near Two Medicine Pass. Keep in mind that this is an uber-long day and requires much physical stamina.

GRIZZLY MOUNTAIN

TRAILHEAD INFORMATION

Follow the trail from the **South Shore Trailhead** (p. 20) to Two Medicine Pass. The trail passes <u>Cobalt Lake</u> and then follows a long ridge over Chief Lodgepole Peak before reaching Two Medicine Pass. Total trail distance is 7.9 miles (12.7 km) with an elevation gain of over 2,518 feet (767 m) due to numerous ups-and-downs on the trail. The off-trail climbing route begins at Two Medicine Pass.

Make it a two-day trip with a campsite at Cobalt Lake.

If pit toilets are available please use them.

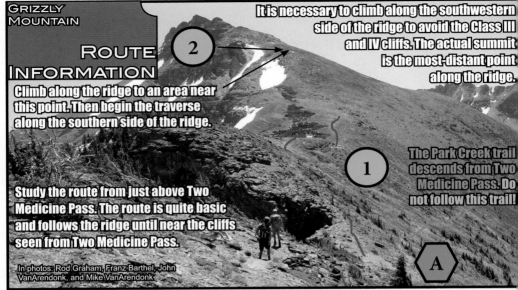

GRIZZLY MOUNTAIN

ROUTE INFORMATION

② It is necessary to climb along the southwestern side of the ridge to avoid the Class III and IV cliffs. The actual summit is the most-distant point along the ridge.

Climb along the ridge to an area near this point. Then begin the traverse along the southern side of the ridge.

Study the route from just above Two Medicine Pass. The route is quite basic and follows the ridge until near the cliffs seen from Two Medicine Pass.

① The Park Creek trail descends from Two Medicine Pass. Do not follow this trail!

In photos: Rod Graham, Franz Barthel, John VanArendonk, and Mike VanArendonk.

A

The lower slopes are consolidated with vegetation and rocks. Ascending through them is not difficult.

Turn around once in a while and enjoy the view.

②

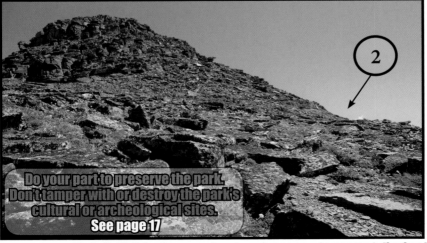

②

This photo shows a recommended transition point from the ridge to the traverse along the southern side.

No toilet? Urinate on rocks, gravel, or snow to prevent digging by animals.

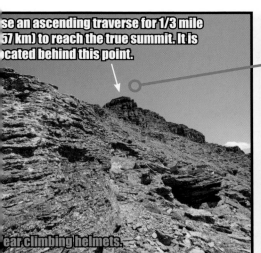

se an ascending traverse for 1/3 mile
57 km) to reach the true summit. It is
cated behind this point.

ear climbing helmets.

Continue across the slope.
There are a few cairns
marking the easiest route,
but do not be concerned
if you cannot
locate them.

The true summit is located
here. Climb towards this
break.

3

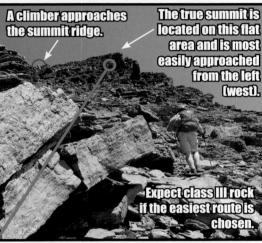

A climber approaches
the summit ridge.

The true summit is
located on this flat
area and is most
easily approached
from the left
(west).

Expect class III rock
if the easiest route is
chosen.

3

here are numerous places to
limb through the final cliffs.

CRUX

Congratulations on a job well
done! This is not an easy climb but
the views are rewarding.

GRIZZLY MOUNTAIN

RETURN ROUTE

Retrace the route back to Two Medicine Pass and the Two Medicine Pass Trail.

Make sure to not stray too far to the east along the ridge there are Class III and IV cliffs that are easily avoided by staying on the west side of the ridge.

Hikers near the Two Medicine Pass Trail.

In photo: Gary Wagener and Roger Bowman

A view to the west from the route.

GRIZZLY MOUNTAIN

OTHER OPTIONS

For most climbers climbing to the summit of Grizzly Mountain and *THEN* returning to the *South Shore Trailhead* (p. 20) is more than enough for one day. But if you want more consider the following:

1) The most common combo-climb is to summit **Painted Tepee Peak** (p. 106) after returning to Chief Lodgepole Peak.

2) An overnight trip could be had by planning ahead and securing a Backcountry Permit. The **Lake Isabel Campground** is 6.1 miles (9.8 km) from Two Medicine Pass. This area can also be reached via a long trail of up the Park Creek Drainage from Walton Ranger Station. It is 14.7 miles (23.6 km) from the Upper Park Campground to the Walton Ranger Station. It is also possible to wade across the Middle Fork of the Flathead River during certain times of the year. There are a lot of bears in this area.

3) Return to the South Shore Trail and take the spur trail to Aster Park.

4) Walk around Two Medicine Lake or walk to the Boat Dock at the inlet of the lake and ride the *Sinopah* back to the **South Shore Trailhead** (p. 20). You can make reservations (*see page 22 for information*) or just pay for a ticket before boarding the boat.

5) Stop and take a cool swim in Cobalt Lake. The snowbank on the far side of the lake indicates just how chilly the lake really is! *Take insect repellent if you plan on hanging out there long.* **The campsites at Cobalt Lake require a permit as well.**

Avoid using re-vegetated areas or blocked trails in campgrounds.

GRIZZLY MOUNTAIN

SUMMIT VIEWS

Rockwell, Flinsch, Painted Tepee, Sinopah, Rising Wolf, Never Laughs, Appistoki, Henry, Ellsworth

Church, Salvage, St. Nicholas, Vigil and Battlement, Caper, Stimson, Rockwell, Flinsch, Rising Wolf

GRIZZLY MOUNTAIN

ROUTE MAP

Legend:

U.S.G.S. Map: Mount Rockwell
Contour Interval = 80 feet

Image provided by mytopo.com
Map Produced by the U.S. Geological Service

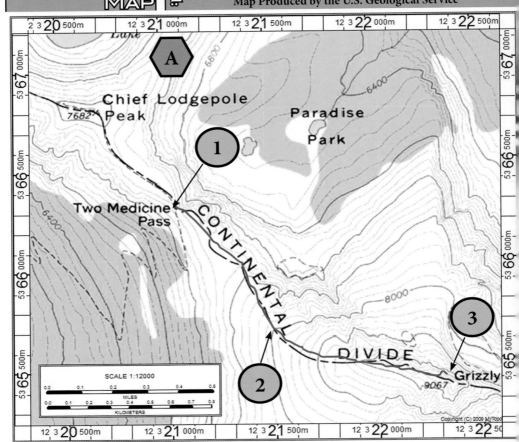

National Geographic Trails Illustrated Maps
Glacier/Waterton Lakes National Parks, Two Medicine (315)
covers the approach to the route for Grizzly Mountain.

Grizzly from the Red Crow Mountain route.

North

M

Declination

MN 14.41° E

ROUTE PROFILE

Elevations and distances are not exact due to variations in the chosen route.

Image provided by mytopo.com

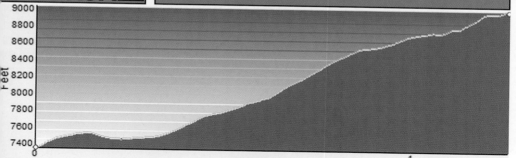

Off-trail statistics from Two Medicine Pass to Grizzly Mountain:
Elevation gained 1,882 feet (573 m) and the total distance is 1.33 miles (2.14 km).

GPS WAYPOINTS

GPS Waypoints are best used in conjunction with a compass, topo map, and common sense.

Relying solely on a GPS for navigation is NOT recommended.

	Latitude	Longitude	Elevation (ft/m)
South Shore Trailhead (p. 20)	48.48313	-113.36822	5,170/1,583
UTM	12 0335 680E	53 67 647N	NAD27
Two Medicine Pass junction	48.46578	-113.38770	5,384/1,641
UTM	12 0335 680E	53 67 647N	NAD27
Rockwell Falls	48.45315	-113.40204	5,439/1,658
UTM	12 0335 680E	53 67 245N	NAD27
Cobalt Lake	48.43476	-113.42460	6,570/2,002
UTM	12 0320 661E	53 67 647N	NAD27
) Two Medicine Pass	48.42633	-113.41892	7,344/2,238
UTM	12 0321 051E	53 66 295N	NAD27
] Northwest Ridge	48.42329	-113.41439	7,600/2,316
UTM	12 0321 376E	53 65 946N	NAD27
] Transition Point On Ridge	48.41985	-113.40960	8,400/2,560
UTM	12 0321 718E	53 65 552N	NAD27
] Summit	48.41839	-113.40188	9,067/2,763
UTM	12 0322 364E	53 65 377N	NAD27

njoy nice summit views!

Mount Rockwell

WEST FACE ROUTE

Photo taken from the air, John VanArendonk photo

AN ENJOYABLE SCRAMBLE THROUGH CLASS III ROCK AFTER A LONGER TRAIL ROUTE TO A PEAK WITH STUNNING VIEWS.

Difficulty: Challenging
GMS Climb Rating: Class III (4) LM
Time Required: 7-10 hours
Season: July to October
One-way Distance: 8 miles / 12.8 km
Elevation Change*: 4,141 feet / 1,262 m

* Elevation Change From Trailhead On Featured Route

Elevation: 9,272 feet / 2,826 m
Rank in Height: 37 of 234
Trailhead: South Shore
U.S.G.S. Topo Map: Mount Rockwell
Trails Illustrated Map: Two Medicine 31
First Recorded Ascent: Norman Clyde o
July 15, 1923

Date Climbed: _____
Climbed With: _____
Notes: _____

Mount Rockwell, like many peaks in the Two Medicine Valley, can be found straddling the Continental Divide. The 37th tallest peak in Glacier National Park is the third-highest featured peak in this volume of "CLIMB GLACIER NATIONAL PARK."

The **West Face Route** begins with an enjoyable stroll through the forested vales on the southern shore of Two Medicine Lake. Stay alert for moose in the swampy areas before reaching Aster Creek. Give them a wide berth as they are totally unpredictable and can be very dangerous. The flat 3.4 miles (5.4 km) of trails allows muscles and joints to get warmed up before reaching the long up-hill grunt beyond Rockwell Falls. The trail, with 5 switchbacks, may seem unrelenting to unfit climbers but the views along upper Rockwell Creek will more than compensate for the pain.

There are some staggering elevations associated with Mount Rockwell. It has a prominence of 2,192 feet (668 m) above the valley floor and the summit stands 1,001 feet (305

m) above the summit of Sinopah Mountain. Beautiful Aurice Lake in the Park Creek Drainage lies 1,947 feet (593 m) below Mount Rockwell's summit cairn.

Another route from Upper Two Medicine Lake has been used in the past to reach the summit of Mount Rockwell but it appears that the game trails once used to "easily" pass through the dense (*read atrocious*") underbrush are no longer being used. *Even animals know when it is horrible.* Saintgrizzly tried it once and he hated it. Don't go there ... unless you enjoy pain.

Mount Rockwell from the Two Medicine Pass Trail.

Follow the trail from the *South Shore Trailhead* (p. 20) to the Two Medicine Pass Junction. At the junction continue to the left on the Two Medicine Pass trail to <u>Cobalt Lake</u>. Approximately 1 mile (1.6 km) from the lake the trail reaches the top of the ridge where the Park Creek Drainage can be seen. It is from this ridge that the off-trail portion of the route begins. Total on-trail distance is about 6.7 miles (10.7 km).

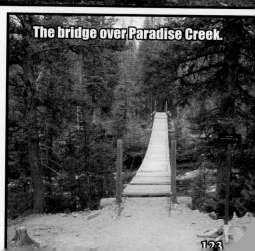

The bridge over Paradise Creek.

Keep group size small.

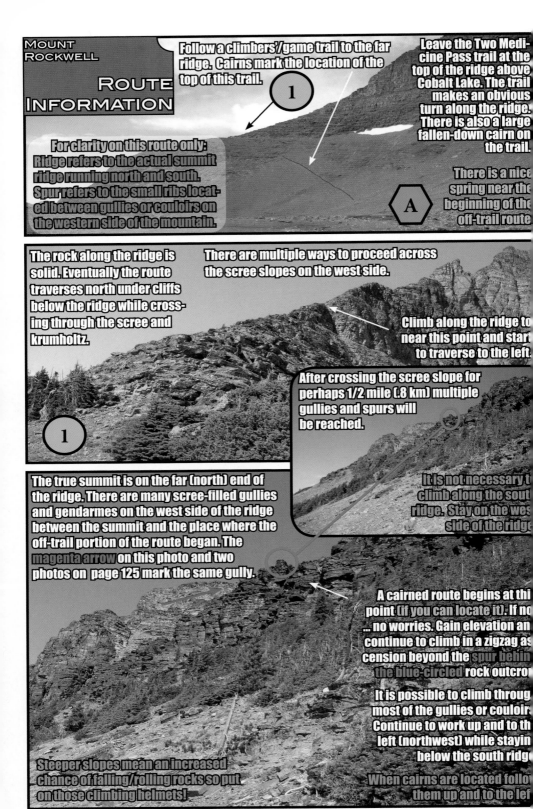

MOUNT ROCKWELL

ROUTE INFORMATION

Follow a climbers'/game trail to the far ridge. Cairns mark the location of the top of this trail.

1

Leave the Two Medicine Pass trail at the top of the ridge above Cobalt Lake. The trail makes an obvious turn along the ridge. There is also a large fallen-down cairn on the trail.

For clarity on this route only: Ridge refers to the actual summit ridge running north and south. Spur refers to the small ribs located between gullies or couloirs on the western side of the mountain.

There is a nice spring near the beginning of the off-trail route

A

The rock along the ridge is solid. Eventually the route traverses north under cliffs below the ridge while crossing through the scree and krumholtz.

There are multiple ways to proceed across the scree slopes on the west side.

Climb along the ridge to near this point and start to traverse to the left.

After crossing the scree slope for perhaps 1/2 mile (.8 km) multiple gullies and spurs will be reached.

1

The true summit is on the far (north) end of the ridge. There are many scree-filled gullies and gendarmes on the west side of the ridge between the summit and the place where the off-trail portion of the route began. The magenta arrow on this photo and two photos on page 125 mark the same gully.

It is not necessary to climb along the south ridge. Stay on the west side of the ridge

A cairned route begins at this point (if you can locate it). If no ... no worries. Gain elevation an continue to climb in a zigzag as cension beyond the spur behin the blue-circled rock outcro

It is possible to climb throug most of the gullies or couloir. Continue to work up and to th left (northwest) while stayin below the south ridg

Steeper slopes mean an increased chance of falling/rolling rocks so put on those climbing helmets!

When cairns are located follo them up and to the le

A definite climber's trail is located on this spur. Stay on the cairned route! Climb up along this spur towards the south ridge. The summit is not far away now! Look for cairns!

The climbers' trail passes through trees and krumholtz along the side of the drainage. The trail meanders through the vegetation and scree until a scree-filled gully below the ridge marked with the magenta arrow can be reached.

In photos: Rod Graham and Chris Rost

Climber on the cairned route.

A cairned route leads through more loose scree and around another spur to the scree-filled gully seen in the above photo as well as the one below.

Climb the spur but stay well below the south ridge to yet another ledge and traverse to the north. A route with many cairns can be found on this spur between two gullies. Follow the spur up to a platform and traverse again to the north (left). This is the final traverse to the ridge below the summit.

Enjoyable Class III (3) climbing.

Enjoy wildlife at a distance.

Two keys to finding a safe route to the summit are locating two nearly flat table-sized rocks.

One is marked with blue in two photos and the upper rock is circled in yellow.

CRUX

The summit.

Traverse below the shelf to the far spur

Chief Lodgepole Peak

Grizzly Mountain

Two Medicine Pass

The Two Medicine Pass trail leads to the summit of Chief Lodgepole Peak. This 7,682 foot (2,341.5 m) peak is located northwest of Two Medicine Pass. The GMS Climb Rating for Chief Lodgepole Peak is Class I (I).

Climb safe ... watch for loose rocks.

②

Follow the cairn-marked route to the pitch below the summit.

Do your part to preserve the park. Don't dig for stuff in the park. See page 17

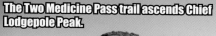

The Two Medicine Pass trail ascends Chief Lodgepole Peak.

The large summit cairn.

is necessary to summit Chief Lodge-
le Peak before reaching Painted Tepee
eak (p. 106) or Grizzly Mountain (p.
14).

otal distance to Chief Lodgepole Peak
om the South Shore Trailhead (p. 20)
5.4 miles (8.6 km) with an elevation
in of 2,518 feet (7.6 km).

The peaks in this photo are Appistoki, Henry, Never Laughs, Ellsworth, and Bearhead.

MOUNT ROCKWELL

RETURN ROUTE

Follow the route back to the Two Medicine Pass Trail and return to the South Shore Trailhead (p. 20).

Other options for descent towards Upper Two Medicine Lake are fraught with intense bushwhacking and are reportedly not overly enjoyable.

Return to this point before looking for the climbers' trail that leads back to the Two Medicine Pass Trail.

MOUNT ROCKWELL

OTHER OPTIONS

This is a long day for most mountaineers.

It may be best to call it a day and head back to the *South Shor* *Trailhead*. However, there are climbing options to consider i you want more!

1) **Chief Lodgepole Peak** (p. 126) and **Painted Tepee Peak** (106) are distinct possibilities after returning to the Two Medicine Pass Trail. There is a b more elevation gain, about 300 feet (91 m), to the summit cairn of Chief Lodgepole Pea but the trail is friendly and the views are astounding! There is even more elevation gai for Painted Tepee Peak.

2) Beyond Chief Lodgepole Peak lies **Grizzly Mountain** (p. 114). This may be a rea stretch for all but the most fit climbers. Adding this summit before (or after) Mount Rock well would be arduous as it would include over 23 miles (37 km) and over 6,000 vertica feet (1,828 m) of elevation gain. *Do not try this unless each member of the group is truly fi*

3) Return to the Two Medicine Trail Junction and hike around <u>Two Medicine Lake</u> b walking 1.8 miles (2.9 km) to the North Shore Trail Junction and then follow the Nort Shore Trail back 3.3 miles (5.3 km) to the *North Shore Trailhead* (p. 20) at the Two Med cine Campground. It would also be necessary to walk back to the Two Medicine Parkin lot unless you plan ahead and leave a vehicle at the *North Shore Trailhead*.

4) The most benign side trip would be a trip of 0.7 miles (1.1 km) to the end of the trail Aster Park. Expect some elevation gain here as well but it is negligible compared to wha has already been done. Look for the sign indicating the junction. <u>Aster Falls</u> is (0.1 mil or 0.2 km) in distance from the South Shore Trail.

Never intentionally approach, feed, or harass wildlife.

MOUNTAINS HAVE DONE THE SPIRITUAL SIDE OF ME MORE GOOD RELIGIOUSLY, AS WELL AS IN MY BODY PHYSICALLY, THAN ANYTHING ELSE IN THE WORLD. NO ONE KNOWS WHO AND WHAT GOD IS UNTIL HE HAS SEEN SOME REAL MOUNTAINEERING AND CLIMBING. REVEREND F. T. WETHERED, 1919

Lone Walker, Stimson, Tinkham, Helen, Flinsch, Red, Rising Wolf

Rising Wolf, Sinopah, Appistoki, Never Laughs, Henry, Ellsworth, Bearhead, Red Crow, Grizzly

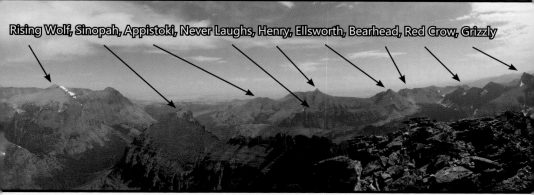

Vigil, St. Nicholas, Battlement, Caper, Cloud Croft, Lone Walker, Stimson

Know and respect regulations and the risks inherent in backcountry travel.

MOUNT ROCKWELL

ROUTE MAP

Legend:

U.S.G.S. Map: Mount Rockwell
Contour Interval = 80 feet

Image provided by mytopo.com
Map Produced by the U.S. Geological Service

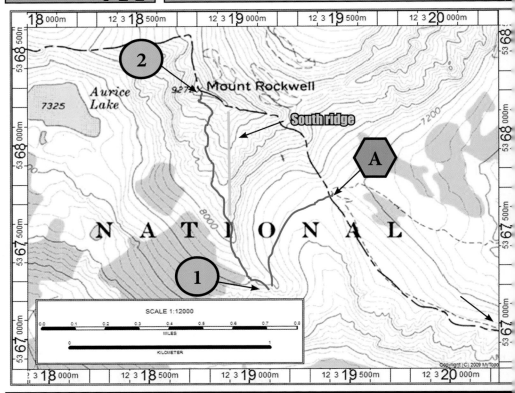

Aurice Lake

7325

Mount Rockwell

South ridge

A

2

1

N A T I O N A L

SCALE 1:12000

MILES

KILOMETER

Copyright (C) 2009 MyTopo

National Geographic Trails Illustrated Maps
Glacier/Waterton Lakes National Parks, Two Medicine (315)
covers the approach to the route for Mount Rockwell.

Aurice Lake from the route.

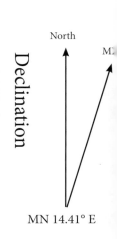

North

M?

Declination

MN 14.41° E

ROUTE PROFILE

Elevations and distances are not exact due to variations in the chosen route.

Image provided by mytopo.com

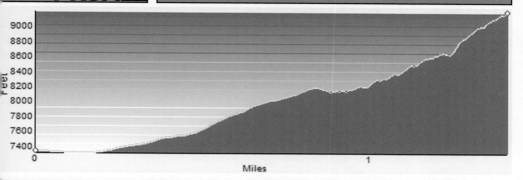

Off-trail statistics from Two Medicine Pass Trail to summit:
Elevation gain is 1,855 feet (565 m) and the total distance is 1.50 miles (2.4 km).

MOUNT
ROCKWELL

GPS WAYPOINTS

GPS Waypoints are best used in conjunction with a compass, topo map, and common sense.

Relying solely on a GPS for navigation is NOT recommended.

	Latitude	Longitude	Elevation (ft/m)
South Shore Trailhead (p. 20)	48.48313	-113.36822	5,170/1,583
UTM	12 0335 680E	53 67 647N	NAD27
Two Medicine Pass junction	48.46578	-113.38770	5,384/1,641
UTM	12 0335 680E	53 67 647N	NAD27
Rockwell Falls	48.45315	-113.40204	5,439/1,658
UTM	12 0335 680E	53 67 245N	NAD27
Cobalt Lake	48.43476	-113.42460	6,570/2,002
UTM	12 0320 661E	53 67 647N	NAD27
A) Begin Off-Trail Route	48.43857	-113.44133	7,336/2,236
UTM	12 0319 437E	53 67 708N	NAD27
1] Bottom of Ridge	48.43626	-113.44797	8,000/2,438
UTM	12 0318 938E	53 67 467N	NAD27
2] Summit	48.44333	-113.45021	9,272/2,826
UTM	12 0318 797E	53 68 258N	NAD27

The jagged ridge to Sinopah Mountain from the summit of Mount Rockwell.

Sinopah Mountian

NORTHEAST RIDGE ROUTE

Photo taken from the Glacier Park Boat Co. Dock Photo by Mike Thompson.

CLIMB ONE OF THE MOST PHOTOGRAPHED PEAKS IN THE PARK

Difficulty: Tolerably Challenging
GMS Climb Rating: Class III (4) MM
Time Required: 6 to 8 hours
Season: July to October
One Way Distance: 5.2 miles / 8.37 km
Elevation Change*: 3,140 feet / 957 m

Elevation: 8,271 feet / 2,521 m
Height In Rank: 147 of 234
Trailhead: South Shore
U.S.G.S. Topo Map: Mount Rockwell
Trails Illustrated Map: Two Medicine 315
First Recorded Ascent: Unknown

* Elevation Change From Trailhead On Featured Route

Date Climbed: _____
Climbed With: _____
Notes: _____

"Saintgrizzly" wrote...

Sinopah Mountain is the crown jewel of the Two Medicine area, not because it is the highest (that, at 9513', would be Rising Wolf Mountain, biggest, or most dramatic, although drama is certainly present!), but because of its striking appearance as it rises from the far-southwestern-pointing-tip of Two Medicine Lake. Sinopah proves to be an irresistible visual magnet, its lake-facing profile an unbroken wall of cliffs sweeping precipitously upward in classic Glacier Park style. Very easy to look at and very photogenic. And a fun mountain to climb.

Sinopah Mountain is the showpiece of the Two Medicine Valley. Its imposing face thrusts out over Two Medicine Lake and is perhaps in the top five of features photographed in Glacier National Park. Perhaps the view of Sinopah Mountain inspired many Native Americans to seek vision quests and find their medicine in this valley.

The Two Medicine Valley has a special significance for the Blackfeet Nation. This beautiful mountain was named for Sinopah the daughter of Lone Walker, a great Blackfeet chief. She was married to Hugh Monroe, who was given the Blackfeet name Rising Wolf. Lone Walker and Rising Wolf Mountains are near Sinopah Mountain. The name "Sinopah" means "Fox Woman" in the Blackfeet language.

This valley has a much more relaxed feeling compared to other areas in the park, but that has not always been so. In the early years the park visitors filled the Two Medicine Valley as they began trail rides from East Glacier. A network of horse trails was established by The Great Northern Railway to show them Glacier's many splendors. The Two Medicine Chalet was built in 1914 but was no longer used after World War II. The chalet was intentionally destroyed in 1956. All that remains of the chalet complex is a small cabin and the dining hall which now serves as the Two Medicine Store.

The rewards of an early start to Sinopah Mountain.

Park near the Two Medicine Lake boat launch and hike 2.3 miles (3.7 km) from the *South Shore Trailhead* (p. 20) on the South Shore Trail to the Two Medicine Pass junction. Spur trails to Paradise Point and Aster Falls will be passed en-route to the Two Medicine Pass Trail junction. There is a suspension bridge crossing Paradise Creek (*except in early or late season when it is removed*).

Continue past the bridge to the Two Medicine Pass Trail junction. Follow the Two Medicine Pass Trail another 1.1 miles (1.8 km) to Rockwell Falls. A log bridge crosses Rockwell Creek. The off-trail route begins on the north side of the creek (*see photo on next page*).

The original name for Sinopah Mountain was "Rising Bull" because it looked lie a buffalo rising. Later it was changed t "Bison" and then J. W. Schultz renamed it "Fox Woman" and finally it was names Sinopah Mountain.

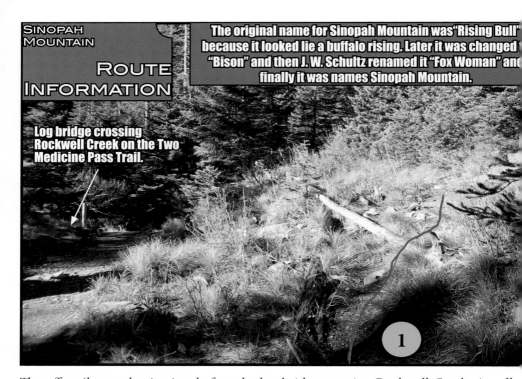

Log bridge crossing Rockwell Creek on the Two Medicine Pass Trail.

1

The off-trail route begins just before the log bridge crossing Rockwell Creek. A well-established climbers' trail ascends beside the cascades and pools of Rockwell Falls. Above the cascade of waterfalls the trail transitions through trees and skirts a stream bed. It th climbs through open scree slopes until reaching the couloir that must be ascended.

Follow the climber's trail as it ascends Rockwell Falls. Spend some time exploring them.

Photos by Mike Thompson

The rocks may be slippery so u caution while exploring Rockw Fal

More people die falling dow waterfalls in the park than by g ting mauled in bear attack

Climbers exploring Rockwell Falls.

In photo: Drew Harris and Ben VanArendonk

Secure food and garbage properly.

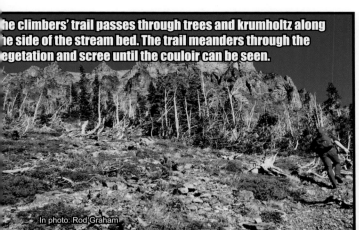

The climbers' trail passes through trees and krumholtz along the side of the stream bed. The trail meanders through the vegetation and scree until the couloir can be seen.

In photo: Rod Graham

Once above the treeline climb near the stream bed. Eventually the climbers' trail disperses but the route to the couloir is obvious.

The slope gets steeper after it passes through the trees. Steeper slopes mean an increased chance of falling/rolling rocks so put on those climbing helmets!

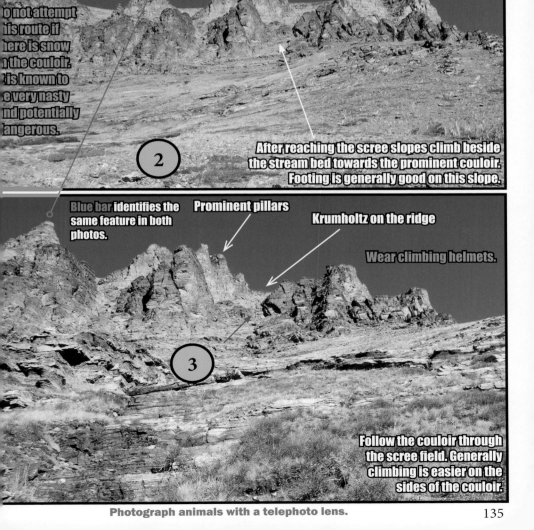

Climb safe ... watch for loose rocks.

Do not attempt this route if there is snow in the couloir. It is known to be very nasty and potentially dangerous.

After reaching the scree slopes climb beside the stream bed towards the prominent couloir. Footing is generally good on this slope.

(2)

Blue bar identifies the same feature in both photos.

Prominent pillars

Krumholtz on the ridge

Wear climbing helmets.

(3)

Follow the couloir through the scree field. Generally climbing is easier on the sides of the couloir.

Photograph animals with a telephoto lens.

Work through the cliff to an area level with the **spires** on the left of the route (*also see photo below as well*).

The **CRUX** is just above a grassy portion on the route and is level with the spires. The route traverses back and forth across the gully and is occasionally marked by cairns. There is no specific best way to climb through this section. Many ways work. Once above the **CRUX** climb towards the formation that looks like the **prow** of a ship.

Wear climbing helmets.

3

CRUX

The prow-like formation

Notice the white bands of rock below the **CRUX**.

4

There are many ways to safely climb through this section of cliffs. This portion of the route is rated Class III (4)

In photos: Rod Graham

Challenge, adventure, discovery, and solitude thrive in the backcountry.

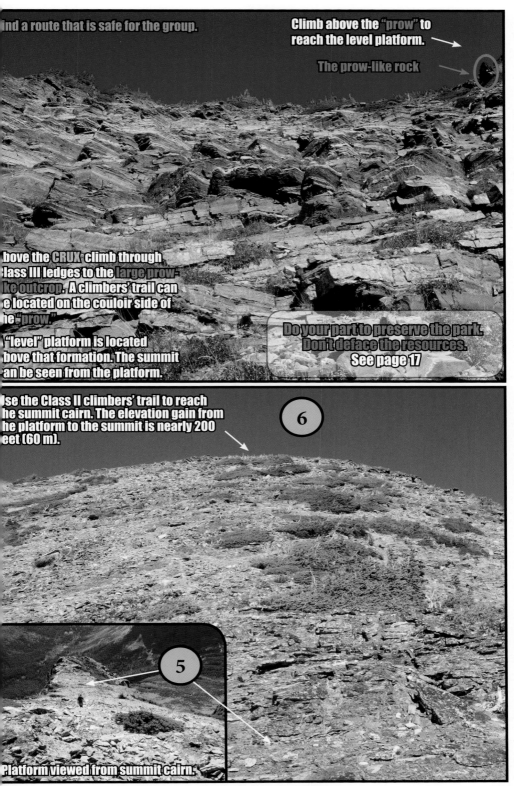

ind a route that is safe for the group.

Climb above the "prow" to reach the level platform. →

The prow-like rock →

bove the CRUX climb through lass III ledges to the large prow-ke outcrop. A climbers' trail can e located on the couloir side of he "prow."

"level" platform is located bove that formation. The summit an be seen from the platform.

Do your part to preserve the park.
Don't deface the resources.
See page 17

se the Class II climbers' trail to reach he summit cairn. The elevation gain from he platform to the summit is nearly 200 eet (60 m).

6

5

Platform viewed from summit cairn.

Remember - a fed bear is a dead bear.

Retrace the route from the summit to the Two Medicine Pa. trail. It is possible to ride the *Sinopah* from the boat dock o the upper end of Two Medicine Lake back to the trailhea One-way tickets can be purchased at the boat dock. It will b necessary to hike extra mileage to the upper end boat launc and frankly it requires more time to hike to the boat dock an wait for the boat than it does just hiking back to the trailhead. If you want to ride the bo. please do so but it requires more time and elevation gain along the hiking trail.

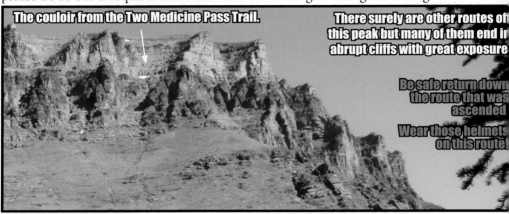

The couloir from the Two Medicine Pass Trail.

There surely are other routes of this peak but many of them end ir abrupt cliffs with great exposure

Be safe return down the route that was ascended

Wear those helmets on this route.

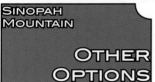

There are no other climbing options that would make sens after climbing Sinopah Mountain. **Do not be tempted to tr and traverse from Sinopah to Mount Rockwell (p. 122). Th. is a difficult and dangerous traverse and requires advance skills.**

Painted Tepee Peak (p. 106), **Chief Lodgepole Peak** (p. 126) and **Grizzly Mountain** (114) are sometimes climbed together in a single day.

1) Enjoy an easy side trip to <u>Aster Falls</u> (0.1 miles or 0.2 km) or <u>Aster Park</u> from the Sout Shore Trail. The distance to the end of the trail is 0.7 miles (1.1 km).

2) A longer hike might include hiking around <u>Two Medicine Lake</u> or even hiking to <u>Upper Two Medicine Lake</u>. It is 4.8 miles (7.7 km) around Two Medicine Lake from the Two Medicine Pass trail junction to the *North Shore Trailhead* (p. 20).

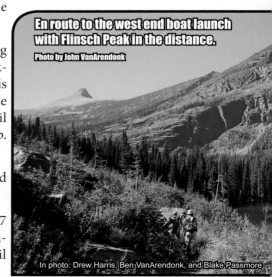

En route to the west end boat launch with Flinsch Peak in the distance.

Photo by John VanArendonk

In photo: Drew Harris, Ben VanArendonk, and Blake Passmore

3) A post-climb trip to <u>Cobalt Lake</u> would be possible with an early start to the day.

Cobalt Lake is an additional 2.3 miles (3.7 km) and about 1,129 feet (344 m)elevation gain on the Two Medicine Pass Trail beyond <u>Rockwell Falls</u>.

SUMMIT VIEWS

THERE ARE 1,557 MILES OF PERENNIAL STREAMS IN GLACIER. MCDONALD CREEK, AT OVER 25 MILES IN LENGTH, IS THE LONGEST STREAM INSIDE OF THE PARK BOUNDARY.

Caper, Lone Walker

Phillips, Helen, Stimson

Grizzly, Painted Tepee, Chief Lodgepole, Rockwell

Spot, Two Medicine Lake, Lower Two Medicine Lake, Scenic Point, Appistoki

Carry adequate food, water, clothing, and the trip essentials.

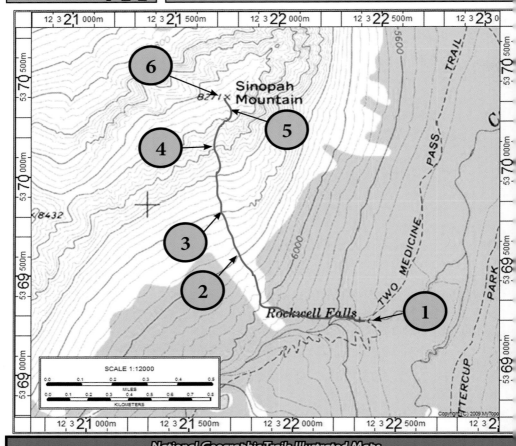

SINOPAH
MOUNTAIN

ROUTE
MAP

Legend:

U.S.G.S. Map: Mount Rockwell
Contour Interval = 80 feet

Image provided by mytopo.com
Map Produced by the U.S. Geological Service

Sinopah Mountain

National Geographic Trails Illustrated Maps
Glacier/Waterton Lakes National Parks, Two Medicine (315)
covers the approach to the route for Sinopah Mountain.

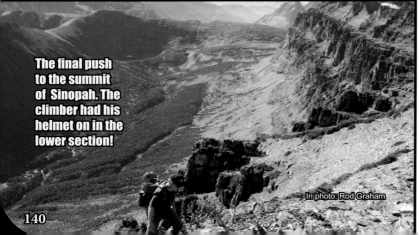

The final push to the summit of Sinopah. The climber had his helmet on in the lower section!

In photo: Rod Graham

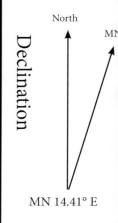

North

MN

Declination

MN 14.41° E

ROUTE
PROFILE

**Elevations and distances are not exact
due to variations in the chosen route.**

Image provided by mytopo.com

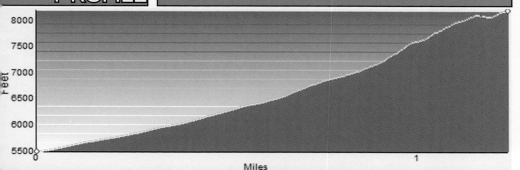

Miles

**Total elevation change from Two Medicine Pass Trail to summit is
2,712 feet (826 m) and the total distance is 1.40 miles (2.25 km).**

GPS
WAYPOINTS

**GPS Waypoints are best used in conjunction with
a compass, topo map, and common sense.**

**Relying solely on a GPS for navigation
is NOT recommended.**

	Latitude	Longitude	Elevation (ft/m)
South Shore Trailhead (p. 20)	48.48313	-113.36822	5,170/1,583
UTM	12 0324 997E	53 72 490N	NAD27
Two Medicine Pass junction	48.46578	-113.38770	5,384/1,641
UTM	12 0323 498E	53 70 607N	NAD27
1] Sinopah Climbers' Trail	48.45315	-113.40204	5,439/1,658
UTM	12 0322 394E	53 69 236N	NAD27
2] Lower Scree Slope	48.45602	-113.41026	6,400/1,950
UTM	12 0321 799E	53 69 575N	NAD27
3] Bottom Of Couloir	48.45959	-113.41198	6,800/2,072
UTM	12 0321 682E	53 69 975N	NAD27
4] Crux	48.46095	-113.41192	7,600/2,316
UTM	12 0321 690E	53 70 126N	NAD27
5] Level Platform	48.46282	-113.41018	8,078/2,462
UTM	12 0321 826E	53 70 330N	NAD27
6] Sinopah Mountain Summit	48.46301	-113.41229	8,271/2,521
UTM	12 0321 826E	53 71 390N	NAD27

Rockwell and points beyond from Sinopah.

142 Lone Walker Mountian

REFERENCE SECTION

UPPER TWO MEDICINE LAKE ROUTE

Photo taken from Upper Two Medicine Lake Trail

PERHAPS THE MOST UNIQUE ROUTE IN THE TWO MEDICINE VALLEY

Difficulty: Challenging
GMS Climb Rating: Class III (4) LM
Time Required: 8-10 hours
Season: July to October
One-way Distance: 8 miles / 12.8 km
Elevation Change*: 3,338 feet / 1,017 m

Elevation: 8,502 feet / 2,591 m
Rank in Height: 123 of 234
Trailhead: North Shore
U.S.G.S. Topo Map: Mount Rockwell
Trails Illustrated Map: Two Medicine 315
First Recorded Ascent: Unknown

* Elevation Change From Trailhead On Featured Route

Date Climbed: _____
Climbed With: _____
Notes: _____
_____
_____
_____
_____
_____
_____

Lone Walker Mountain may be the most difficult peak to access in the Two Medicine Valley. No trails reach its base and the approaches involve either a bushwhack, a long ascent or a large elevation gain and loss prior to reaching the summit. If Lone Walker is on the menu prepare for a challenging-yet-extremely-rewarding day in Glacier.

The Upper Two Medicine Lake Route includes a trail hike (which can be made shorter by riding the *Sinopah*), wading around Upper Two Medicine Lake, and 3,100 feet (944 m) of climbing. Another option is to traverse from the Two Medicine Pass Trail below **Mount Rockwell** after a 6.5 mile hike that includes passing beautiful Cobalt Lake. The route from **Mount Helen** involves reaching Dawson Pass, climbing 940 feet (286 m) to Mount Helen, loosing 1,500 feet and then regain that much again to reach the summit of Lone Walker. None of these routes are easy. The Upper Two Medicine Lake route has the least trail distance and elevation gain. The only thing it potentially has more of is bushwhack and most of that can be avoided by bringing wading shoes and walking along the shore of Upper Two Medicine Lake.

According to park legend, Chief Lone Walker was the father of Sinopah who married Rising Wolf, a white man who was adopted into the Blackfoot nation. It is fitting that these peaks be found in close proximity to this day.

The Upper Two Medicine Lake Trail

Check out Lone Walker if you are looking for isolation in this generally accessible valley. Enjoy incredible views into the isolated Nyack, Park and Coal Creek drainages. On a clear day many of the park's well known peaks can be seen. A trip to the summit of Lone Walker Mountain is sure to impact climbers who put the effort to reach this peak.

Get an early start from the *North Shore Trailhead* (p. 20) and walk 3.3 (5.3 km) miles to Upper Two Medicine Lake. **Carefully read all of the signs at each junction. Carry wading shoes for this route!**

This climb can be made 6 miles shorter by taking the *Sinopah* in both directions. Reserve a spot on the boat if desired. Plan on using the 9:00 a.m. departure. It is also possible to use the boat on the return route. The last departure is at 5:20 p.m. Bring cash to pay for the boat ride! See page 22.

Another option is to reserve a campsite at __Upper Two Medicine Lake__ and make this a two-day trip. This could make the climb much more enjoyable for those who appreciate staying in Glacier's backcountry campgrounds.

Visit the park's web page to make advanced reservations or test your luck and stop in a Backcountry Ranger Station prior to starting the trip.

If you travel off trail, walk abreast and select the most durable route.

LONE WALKER MOUNTAIN

ROUTE INFORMATION

Follow the north shoreline of Upper Two Medicine Lake from the end of the hiking trail.

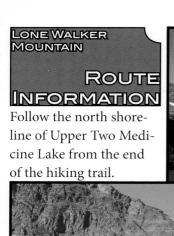

Stash your wading shoes for the return wade. There is no need to carry wet shoes to the summit.

Some critters like to chew on gear so stash intelligently.

Walk along the shoreline until reaching the bottom of this scree field.

1

Stay away from the cliffs, instead climb above them.

Study the route from below the saddle. Locate the Class III (4) **ramp** to the south of the **prominent steep-black couloir**. It will take some route finding to find a way through that is safe for the group.

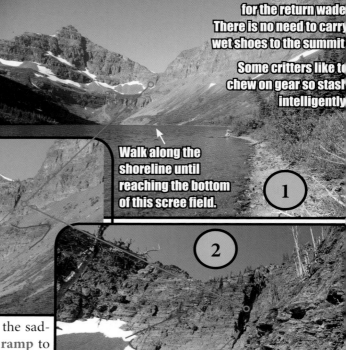

2

Blue bar indicates same feature in three photos.

Work up and to the right on this ramp. Look for a safe route.

In photo: Read Vaughan

If a goat trail can be located follow it through the cliffs.

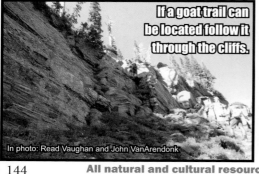

In photo: Read Vaughan and John VanArendonk

The slope moderates above the cliffs.

2

Walk up the ridge from the saddle.

Stay to the right (west) of the ridge or on the ridge while climbing around the small sets of cliffs along the summit ridge.

Eventually the summit will be seen above a large talus-filled bowl. Stay near the ridge for easier climbing.

The CRUX is located to the left (East) of this notch in the skyline.

To locate the CRUX look for a lichen-covered wall with a **small keyhole**. The **climber** in the photo is below a small couloir which is scrambled through to reach solid Class III (4) scrambling which leads to the summit. There surely are other ways to the summit but this route is enjoyable and has minimal amounts of scree.

From the CRUX climb to the east (left) and then ascend up and to the right. Cairns mark this portion of the route.

It is also possible to traverse west and climb the scree field on the south side of the summit.

Notch in the skyline.

The small couloir that leads to the Class III (4) scrambling.

CRUX

In photo: Rod Graham

In photo: Read Vaughan

There are many ways to reach the final ridge. Find a safe way for your group.

The summit ridge is located just above the climber.

Once on the ridge climb to the left!

In photo: John VanArendonk

Carefully scramble along the ridge to the summit.

3

In photo: John VanArendonk

...erries and fish for personal consumption only.

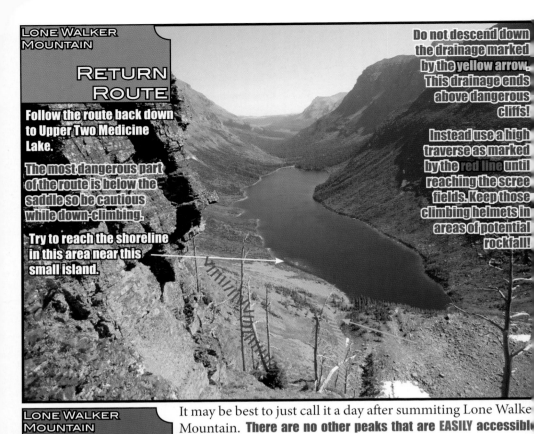

LONE WALKER MOUNTAIN

RETURN ROUTE

Follow the route back down to Upper Two Medicine Lake.

The most dangerous part of the route is below the saddle so be cautious while down-climbing.

Try to reach the shoreline in this area near this small island.

Do not descend down the drainage marked by the yellow arrow. This drainage ends above dangerous cliffs!

Instead use a high traverse as marked by the red line until reaching the scree fields. Keep those climbing helmets in areas of potential rockfall!

LONE WALKER MOUNTAIN

OTHER OPTIONS

It may be best to just call it a day after summiting Lone Walke Mountain. **There are no other peaks that are EASILY accessible from its location.** The *Sinopah* tour boat is a great way to trave both directions on Two Medicine Lake. This saves about miles of trail hiking and quite a bit of time. Carry cash to pa for the ride! Make sure you have a trail map along to work ou all of the trail junctions!

If you are a glutton for punishment and want more consider the following options:

1) After returning to the Two Medicine Pass Trail hike up the Dawson Pass Trail to N Name Lake. This would add a bit of mileage but not much elevation. Remember that yo still have to return to the trailhead. *There is a campground here.*

2) Enjoy an easy side trip to <u>Twin Falls from the Upper Two Medicine Lake Trail.</u> A shor trip up a spur trail leads to this intriguing double waterfall.

3) A longer hike might include hiking around <u>Two Medicine Lake</u>. The trail travels 1. miles (2.9 km) from the from the Dawson Pass Trail junction to the Two Medicine Pas Junction and another 2.3 miles (3.7 km) to the *South Shore Trailhead* (p. 20). It is no necessary to retrace the route to the Dawson Pass Trail junction just make sure you are o the South Shore Trail headed southeast toward the Two Medicine Trail junction.

4) A post-climb swim could be in order at Two Medicine Lake. Look for a likely spot t take a quick dip along the Dawson Pass Trail on the way back to the *North Shore Trai head* (p. 20). *Remember this is a popular trail and receives a lot of traffic!*

Choose durable surfaces such as rock, snow, gravel, or dry grasses for travel.

GOING-TO-THE-SUN HIGHWAY'S EAST SIDE
TUNNEL IS 408 FEET LONG AND THE WEST
SIDE TUNNEL IS 192 FEET LONG.

Rockwell, Summit, Despair, Brave Dog, Vigil, Battlement

Caper, Mount St. Nicholas, Cloudcroft Peaks, Peril, Great Northern, Phillips

Phillips, Tinkham, Morgan, Flinsch, Helen, Rising Wolf

Never make alterations to tent sites or natural features.

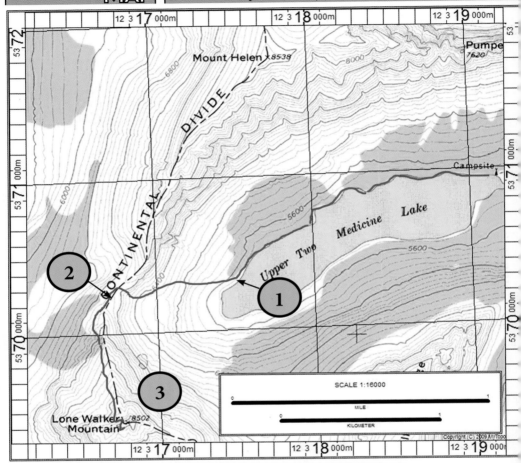

LONE WALKER MOUNTAIN

ROUTE MAP

Legend:

U.S.G.S. Map: Mount Rockwell
Contour Interval = 80 feet

Image provided by mytopo.com
Map Produced by the U.S. Geological Service

Mount Helen ×8538

DIVIDE

Pumpe
7620

Campsite

6800

8000

CONTINENTAL

6600

6000

5600

5600

Upper Two Medicine Lake

2

1

3

Lone Walker ×8502
Mountain

SCALE 1:16000

MILE

KILOMETER

Copyright (C) 2009 MyTopo

National Geographic Trails Illustrated Maps
Glacier/Waterton Lakes National Parks, Two Medicine (315)
covers the approach to the route for Lone Walker Mountain.

Looking down the route to the saddle.

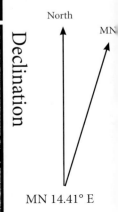

North

MN

Declination

MN 14.41° E

Elevations and distances are not exact due to variations in the chosen route.

Image provided by mytopo.com

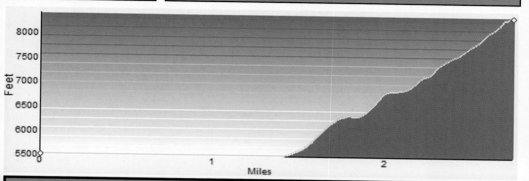

Off-trail statistics from Upper Two Medicine Lake to Lone Walker summit: Elevation gained 3,265 feet (995 m) and the total distance is 3 miles (4.8 km).

GPS Waypoints are best used in conjunction with a compass, topo map, and common sense.

Relying solely on a GPS for navigation is NOT recommended.

	Latitude	Longitude	Elevation (ft/m)
North Shore Trailhead (p. 20)	48.48858	-113.36626	5,129/1,563
UTM	12 0325 162E	53 73 029N	NAD27
[1] Upper Two Medicine Lake Shore	48.46806	-113.46964	5,508/1,678
UTM	12 0317 423E	53 70 252N	NAD27
[2] Helen - Lone Walker Saddle	48.46108	-113.47868	6,854/2,089
UTM	12 0316 756E	53 70 299N	NAD27
[3] Summit	48.45324	-113.47791	8,502/2,591
UTM	12 0316 758E	53 69 425N	NAD27

Mount Phillips

Lone Walker Mountain from the air.
John VanArendonk photo.

Do your part to preserve the park.
Don't enter a protected/closed area.
See page 17

149

Mount Helen

DAWSON PASS ROUTE

Photo taken from Flinsch Peak
Photo by Mike Thompson

GREAT VIEWS AFTER A LONG TRAIL HIKE BUT WORTH THE EFFORT

Difficulty: Challenging
GMS Climb Rating: Class II (3) LM
Time Required: 7-10 hours
Season: Late June to October
One-way Distance: 7.4 miles / 11.9 km
Elevation Change*: 3,406 feet / 1,038 m

Elevation: 8,538 feet / 2,602 m
Rank in Height: 119 of 234
Trailhead: North Shore
U.S.G.S. Topo Map: Mount Rockwell
Trails Illustrated Map: Two Medicine 315
First Recorded Ascent: Unknown

* Elevation Change From Trailhead On Featured Route

Date Climbed: _____
Climbed With: _____
Notes: _____
_____
_____
_____
_____
_____
_____

Mount Helen is not a major peak in the Two Medicine Valley. Its main significance is a result of its position on the Continental Divide. This peak is often overlooked due to its nearest neighbor, Flinsch Peak, being a much more desirable destination for climbers. Mount Helen is a worthy destination for climbers who prefer less exposure.

The hike to Dawson Pass is sure to be a highlight for many Glacier National Park visitors. The trail travels along the northern shore of Two Medicine Lake before entering <u>Bighorn Basin</u>. A short side trip to <u>No Name Lake</u> rewards hikers with beautiful views. Riding the *Sinopah* shortens the trip and is less tiresome for most hikers.

From Helen's summit the Two Medicine Valley sprawls eastward with picturesque views as valleys make a seamless transition into the Great Plains of Montana. With a pair of binoculars it is possible to see trout rising on the surface of Upper Two Medicine Lake over 3,000 feet (914 m) below Mount Helen's summit. Mount Phillips and Mount Stimson dominate the views to the west and northwest. The Continental Divide snakes across numerous summits in its never-ending quest for northern and southern borders.

One of the more interesting features seen on the route to Helen is Pumpelly Pillar. The pillar stands 7,600 feet above sea level and requires Class IV & V climbing and excellent route finding skills. The pillar is usually approached from the Upper Two Medicine Lake Trail. This route is for intermediate to advanced climbers and is not featured in "CLIMB GLACIER NATIONAL PARK."

Mount Helen and Flinsch Peak anchor a fantastic view from Rising Wolf Mountain.

The Dawson Pass Trail travels 6.4 miles (10.3 km) from the *North Shore Trailhead* (p. 20) to <u>Dawson Pass</u>. Follow the trail to the left (southwest) at the junction past the footbridge. The initial portion of the hike requires little elevation change and goes quickly. The majority of the 2,400 feet (731 m) of elevation gain is from the trail junction at <u>No Name Lake</u> to Dawson Pass. From the No Name Lake junction the trail gains 1,600 feet (487 m) in 1.8 miles (2.8 km). Make sure you are doing plenty of "heybearing" on the trails! This is bear country, they use the hiking trails and especially enjoy huckleberries in the fall!

Riding the *Sinopah* reduces the overall mileage of this climb by 6 miles. It is a great option if the schedule works for the group. Sometimes timing is an issue so plan thoughtfully!

There are no reliable water sources above No Name Lake so plan accordingly!

Climbers with time to spare can reserve a backcountry campsite at <u>No Name Lake</u> and make this a two-day trip.

Avoid fragile vegetation and saturated soils.

Take a short rest at Dawson Pass to ponder the magnificen views!

The climb to Helen's summit consists of 1,017 feet (309 m) o hiking and a short section of scrambling, *if desired*, along th ridgeline. There is one set of crumbly Class III cliffs that ca be avoided by walking on the west side of the ridge.

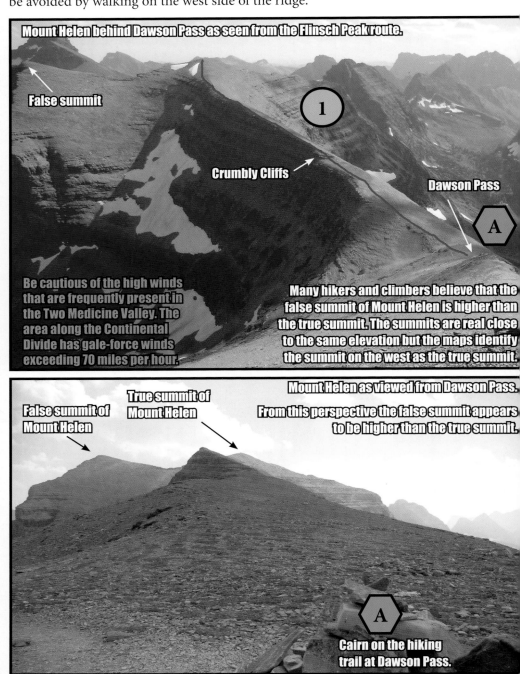

Mount Helen behind Dawson Pass as seen from the Flinsch Peak route.

False summit

1

Crumbly Cliffs

Dawson Pass

A

Be cautious of the high winds that are frequently present in the Two Medicine Valley. The area along the Continental Divide has gale-force winds exceeding 70 miles per hour.

Many hikers and climbers believe that the false summit of Mount Helen is higher than the true summit. The summits are real close to the same elevation but the maps identify the summit on the west as the true summit.

Mount Helen as viewed from Dawson Pass.

From this perspective the false summit appears to be higher than the true summit.

False summit of Mount Helen

True summit of Mount Helen

A

Cairn on the hiking trail at Dawson Pass.

WHILE CAMPING:

This is the only portion of the route with climbing possibilities (which will be very short-lived). Climb the through the easy Class II (3) cliffs or walk around on the right (west) side of this small set of cliffs.

Crumbly Cliffs

Walk around this side.

The rock along the ridge is easier to walk on than the rock on the slope.

On the western side of the ridge the rock is loose and therefore is more difficult to climb through.

A climbers'/goat trail leads up the route.

In photos: Joey Gardner and Matt Fitzwater

1

Continue walking near the ridge to the summit.

Eventually the goat trail starts to traverse below the summit.

It is necessary to climb to the ridge and walk up the ridge to the summit.

Do your part to preserve the park. Don't disturb the park resources.
See page 17

MOUNT HELEN

RETURN ROUTE

Trace the route back to Dawson Pass and return to the North Shore Trailhead (p. 20).

Another option is to ride the *Sinopah* back to the trailhead. The boat leaves the upper end of Two Medicine Lake at 3:20 p.m. and 5:20 p.m. Purchase tickets at the kiosk by the South Shore Trailhead (p. 20).

MOUNT HELEN

OTHER OPTIONS

There are few sensible options left after climbing Mount Helen. It may be best to head back and enjoy a ride on the *Sinopah*.

No Name Lake and Two Medicine Lake from the Mount Helen Ridge.

1) The most obvious is to summit **Flinsch Peak** (p. 158) via the South Slope Route.

2) It is also possible to reach **Rising Wolf Mountain** (p. 168) from Dawson Pass. Climbing Helen and then Rising Wolf adds a significant amount of hours to the day and is no the normal approach for Rising Wolf. This guidebook suggests that Rising Wolf Mountain be climbed via the *West Ridge Route* and **THEN** traverse to Dawson Pass on the return route rather than down climb dangerous cliffs on the west face of Rising Wolf Mountain

3) It is also possible to walk north along the Continental Divide toward **Mount Morgan** (p. 180). Turn around at a set turn-around time and return to the *North Shore Trailhead* (p. 20) or the boat launch on the west end of Two Medicine Lake or ….

4) Follow the trail as it extends to Pitamakan Pass before dropping down into the Dr Fork Drainage near Old Man Lake. All that can be said here is that it is "mostly" down-hil and quite beautiful on the 11.2 miles (18 km) walk back to the *North Shore Trailhead* (20). This requires over 18 miles (29 km) of trail time plus off-trail distance and elevation gain. This trail hike in-and-of-itself is a big undertaking for most hikers.

Cook and eat only in the designated food preparation area.

SUMMIT VIEWS

WILL ALLOWS YOU TO CLIMB SUMMITS; WITHOUT WILL YOU STAY AT THE BASE OF THE MOUNTAIN. - CHINESE SAYING

All **Summit View** photos for Mount Helen were taken during the August 2011 fire season which caused the haze seen in these photos. On a clear day the views are outstanding!

Rockwell, Vigil, Salvage, Lone Walker, Church, Caper, St. Nicholas

Cloud Croft Peaks, Phillips, Stimson

Lupfer Glacier

Pumpelly Glacier, Nyack Valley, Tinkham, Morgan, Flinsch

Never cook or eat in your tent.

ROUTE MAP

Legend:

U.S.G.S. Map: Mount Rockwell
Contour Interval = 80 feet

Image provided by mytopo.com
Map Produced by the U.S. Geological Service

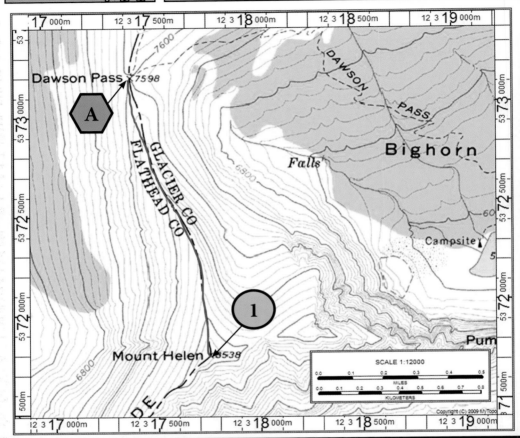

Dawson Pass 7598

A

GLACIER CO

FLATHEAD CO

DAWSON PASS

Bighorn

Falls

6800

Campsite

1

Mount Helen 8538

Pum

SCALE 1:12000

MILES

KILOMETERS

6800

Copyright (C) 2009 MyTopo

National Geographic Trails Illustrated Maps
Glacier/Waterton Lakes National Parks, Two Medicine (315)
covers the approach to the route for Mount Helen.

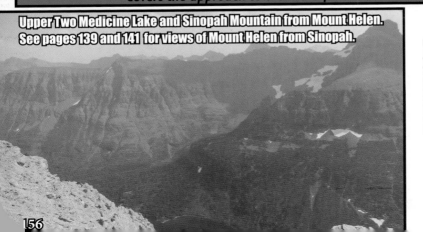

Upper Two Medicine Lake and Sinopah Mountain from Mount Helen.
See pages 139 and 141 for views of Mount Helen from Sinopah.

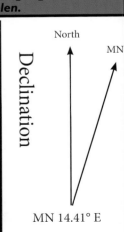

North

MN

Declination

MN 14.41° E

ROUTE PROFILE

Elevations and distances are not exact due to variations in the chosen route.

Image provided by mytopo.com

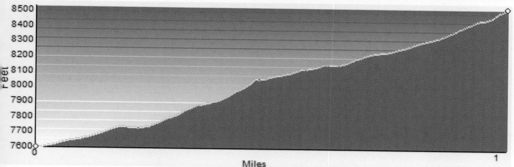

Total elevation change from Dawson Pass to the Mount Helen summit is 1,017 feet (309 m) and the total distance is 1.04 miles (1.67 km).

MOUNT HELEN

GPS WAYPOINTS

GPS Waypoints are best used in conjunction with a compass, topo map, and common sense.

Relying solely on a GPS for navigation is NOT recommended.

	Latitude	Longitude	Elevation (ft/m)
North Shore Trailhead (p. 20)	48.48858	-113.36626	5,129/1,563
UTM	12 0325 162E	53 73 029N	NAD27
Two Medicine Pass Trail Jct.	48.47786	-113.41842	5,238/1,596
UTM	12 0321 270E	53 72 021N	NAD27
No Name Lake Jct.	48.48113	-113.44484	6,000/1,828
UTM	12 0319 331E	53 72 446N	NAD27
A) Dawson Pass	48.48715	-113.47087	7,595/2,315
UTM	12 0317 427E	53 73 177N	NAD27
] Summit	48.47404	-113.46564	8,538/2,602
UTM	12 0317 768E	53 71 771N	NAD27

Mount Helen from the Dawson Pass Trail. The true summit is to the right of the large snowfield.

Flinsch Peak

SOUTH SLOPE ROUTE

and

EAST RIDGE ROUTE

Photo taken from Sinopah Mountain

VIEWS DO NOT GET MUCH BETTER THAN THIS!

Difficulty: Challenging
GMS Climb Rating: Class III (3) LM
Time Required: 8 - 10 hours
Season: Late June to October
One-way Distance: 7.7 miles / 12.4 km
Elevation Change*: 4,096 feet / 1,248 m

Elevation: 9,225 feet / 2,812 meters
Rank in Height: 41 of 234
Trailhead: North Shore
U.S.G.S. Topo Map: Mount Rockwell
Trails Illustrated Map: Two Medicine 31
First Recorded Ascent: Unknown

* Elevation Change From Trailhead On Featured Route

Date Climbed: _____
Climbed With: _____
Notes: _____
_____
_____
_____
_____
_____
_____

"Saintgrizzly" wrote...

The trail climbs steadily, with Flinsch coming more and more into focus, the last bit of elevation gain to the pass leaves the forest behind, the scene opens as it climbs, Flinsch is now visible in its entirety, and then you reach the pass ... and if you're like me, at that point you stop, not even thinking to take off your pack; stop, and just look. And say something inspirational to fill the moment, like a softly spoken, "Wow ..." Or, even after a lifetime of seeing, "... oh-my-goodness these mountains are ... BIG."

Then (if you're like me) you remember you have a camera, have enough sense to drop your pack, and start running from one end of the pass to the other, because every few steps seems to bring something even more—or at least as worthy as what was just a few feet ago - wonderful of which to take a picture. Dawson Pass does that to you ...

And still, up and away in the near distance: the horn of Flinsch Peak.

Flinsch Peak cuts a stunning figure on the Continental Divide north of Dawson Pass. This peak is a glacial horn like Reynolds Mountain, Flinsch Peak presents opportunities for spectacular views that are obtainable for most mountaineers who posses a degree of fortitude and endurance. This climb is more strenuous than Reynolds Mountain due to the length of the approach and required elevation gain.

It would seem that Flinsch Peak is surrounded by a lot of lakes in an area that is well known for its spectacular lakes. Oldman Lake sits in the Dry Fork basin northeast of the peak, Young Man Lake lies directly east of the summit. To go along with the human theme; Boy Lake sparkles further to the east. No Name Lake and Two Medicine Lake can also be seen from the summit. That's a lot of fishing water to explore if you are so inclined!

Flinsch Peak is often summited in the same day as Rising Wolf Mountain but it certainly does not need to be done that way. A more leisurely day could be had by riding the Glacier Park Boat Company's launch, *Sinopah*, from the Two Medicine Boat Launch and then approach Dawson Pass from the west end of the lake. This would cut of a good 2 hours of trail time **IF** you can get the timing right for riding the Sinopah both ways.

FLINSCH PEAK

TRAILHEAD INFORMATION

Hike 6.4 miles (10.3 km) from the *North Shore Trailhead* (p. 20) to Dawson Pass. Follow the Dawson Pass Trail to the left (southwest) at the junction past the footbridge. The initial portion of the hike has little elevation change and goes quickly. Stay to the right at all subsequent junctions.

The majority of the 2,400 feet (731 m) of elevation gain is from the trail junction at No Name Lake to Dawson Pass. The trail gains 1,600 feet (487 m) in 1.8 miles (2.8 km).

There are no reliable water sources above No Name Lake so plan accordingly!

Another option is to reserve a backcountry campsite at **No Name Lake** and make this a two-day trip.

Store all food, cookware, toiletries, and garbage in a approved food-storage device. 159

ROUTE INFORMATION

Reaching the summit of Flinsch Peak requires 1,630 feet (496 m) of elevation gain from Dawson Pass. Some of the elevation is gained on the hiking trail.

1

A

The view of the route to Flinsch Peak from the Dawson Pass Trail.

From the trail climb through the generally consolidated scree field until near the point indicated with the yellow arrow.

The rock becomes less stable and the scree field loosens up as elevation is gained.

Locate a climbers' trail and climb through the loose scree to the right (east) side of the yellow lichen-covered outcropping.

The CRUX is located on the right (east) side of the yellow lichen-covered outcrop.

In photo: Micah Tinkham and Mike Thompson

Do not throw garbage or food scraps in the pit toilets.

Climb through the Class III cliffs and scree ledges below the yellow lichen-covered outcrop.

The **CRUX** is located in this corner behind the outcrop.

CRUX

The rock on this route is quite loose. Carefully check all hand and foot holds before relying on them.

Also guard against releasing any loose rock and debris on those who might be climbing below.

In photo: Mike Thompson

It is obvious where the summit is but believe it or not there are even more cairns on the ridge leading to the summit.

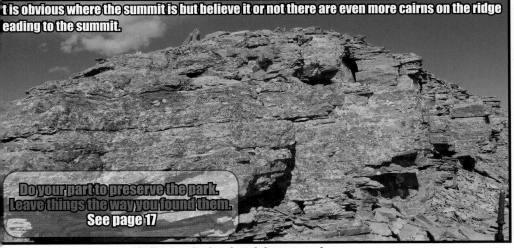

Do your part to preserve the park. Leave things the way you found them.

See page 17

Collect only dead and down wood.

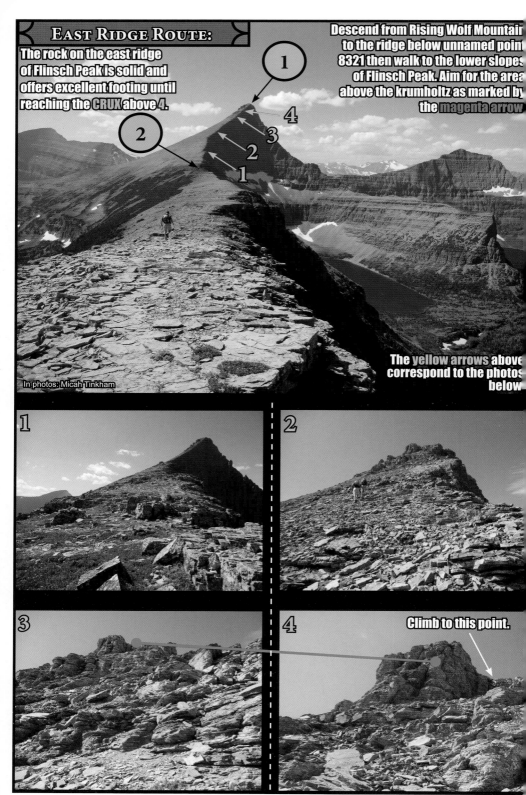

EAST RIDGE ROUTE:
The rock on the east ridge of Flinsch Peak is solid and offers excellent footing until reaching the CRUX above 4.

Descend from Rising Wolf Mountain to the ridge below unnamed point 8321 then walk to the lower slopes of Flinsch Peak. Aim for the area above the krumholtz as marked by the magenta arrow

The yellow arrows above correspond to the photos below

In photos: Micah Tinkham

Climb to this point.

Store other gear in your tent.

Climb through enjoyable Class III rock.

Climb to this point.

Photo by Mike Thompson
In photo: Blake Passmore

The left side of the gully is quite loose. There are other routes through Class III rock on the right side of the gully. Watch for loose rock and helmets are recommended!

(1)

CRUX

In photo: Micah Tinkham

The summit is just beyond the top of the gully.

A spare stuff sack and a rope at least 25 feet long are needed for hanging food.

RETURN ROUTE

The most obvious return route is back to the ***North Sho***
Trailhead (p. 20). Carefully down-climb through the rott
rock on Flinsch Peak and return to the Dawson Pass Trail.
cautious on this loose rock while descending. Wear a climbi
helmet until well clear of the dangerous slope.

If you are planning on catching the *Sinopah* remember th
the boats depart at 3:20 p.m. and 5:20 p.m. from the Boat Landing at the west end of T
Medicine Lake. It is 4.4 miles (7 km) from Dawson Pass to the Boat Landing so plan a
cordingly!

If you happen to miss the boat (*no pun intended*) plan on an additional 3.3 miles (5.3 k
of hiking along the North Shore Trail. The trail is relatively flat and passes quickly but t
extra miles could be a disappointment if counting on an enjoyable dinner at one of t
fine restaurants in East Glacier. Make sure to be "heybearing" along the trail!

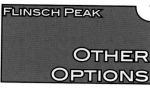

OTHER OPTIONS

1) **Mount Helen** (p. 150) is frequently climbed in combin
tion with Flinsch Peak.

2) It is also possible to summit **Rising Wolf Mountain** (p. 16
via the ***South Face Route*** prior to summiting Flinsch.

3) Another option is to continue on the Dawson Pass Trail to Pitamakan Pass and follo
the Pitamakan Pass Trail past Old Man Lake and return to the ***North Shore Trailhead*** (
20). Total trail distance from Dawson Pass is 11.2 miles (18 km) and the round-trip tra
distance would be 17.9 miles (28.8 km) **WITHOUT** any off-trail routes. **Mount Morga**
(p. 180) is a fun scramble from the Pitamakan Pass Overlook.

4) Return to the No Name Lake Junction and walk the short distance (0.2 miles / 320 m
to enjoys the views while swatting bugs (*sometimes*) at No Name Lake.

5) Return to the South Shore Trail Junction and follow the trail signs to Twin Falls. Th
requires relative flat trail time. Return to the ***North Shore Trailhead*** (p. 20) or ride th
Sinopah.

6) It is also possible to continue along the South Shore Trail and return to the ***South Sho***
Trailhead (p. 20). Total distance from the South Shore Trail Junction is 4.1 miles (6.6 km
Bring a trail map to help navigate through the numerous junctions and spur trails on the trail.

A rather photogenic view of Flinsch Peak and Mount Morgan from the ridge west of Rising Wolf Mountain.

In photo: Mike Thompson and Micah Tinkham

SUMMIT VIEWS

THE CONTINENTAL DIVIDE TRAIL IN GLACIER NATIONAL PARK IS 110 MILES (177 KM) IN LENGTH.

Lupfer Glacier, Phillips, Pinchot, Stimson, Tinkham, Morgan

Rising Wolf, Appistoki, Henry, Sinopah, Grizzly, Rockwell

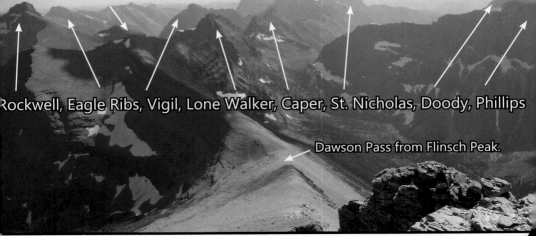

Helen

Rockwell, Eagle Ribs, Vigil, Lone Walker, Caper, St. Nicholas, Doody, Phillips

Dawson Pass from Flinsch Peak.

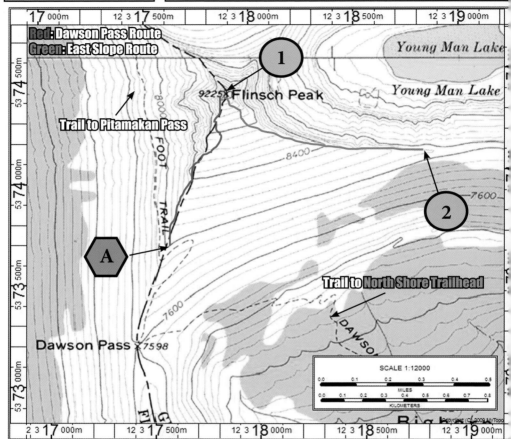

FLINSCH PEAK

ROUTE MAP

Legend:

U.S.G.S. Map: Mount Rockwell
Contour Interval = 80 feet

Image provided by mytopo.com
Map Produced by the U.S. Geological Service

Red: Dawson Pass Route
Green: East Slope Route

Trail to Pitamakan Pass

9225 Flinsch Peak

Young Man Lake

Young Man Lake

Trail to North Shore Trailhead

Dawson Pass 7598

SCALE 1:12000

National Geographic Trails Illustrated Maps
Glacier/Waterton Lakes National Parks, Two Medicine (315)
covers the approaches to the routes for Flinsch Peak.

Its an intelligent idea to wear a helmet on upper section of this route!

In photo: Mike Thompson

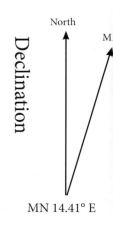

North

M

Declination

MN 14.41° E

ROUTE PROFILE

Elevations and distances are not exact due to variations in the chosen route.
Image provided by mytopo.com

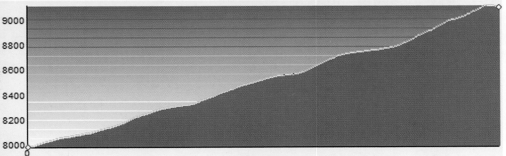

Miles

Total off-trail elevation change from Dawson Pass Trail to Flinsch Peak summit is 1,150 feet (350 m) and the total distance is .67 miles (1 km).

LINSCH PEAK

GPS WAYPOINTS

GPS Waypoints are best used in conjunction with a compass, topo map, and common sense.

Relying solely on a GPS for navigation is NOT recommended.

		Latitude	Longitude	Elevation (ft/m)
North Shore Trailhead (p. 20)		48.48858	-113.36626	5,129/1,563
	UTM	12 0325 162E	53 73 029N	NAD27
Two Medicine Pass Trail Jct.		48.47786	-113.41842	5,238/1,596
	UTM	12 0321 270E	53 72 021N	NAD27
No Name Lake Jct.		48.48113	-113.44484	6,000/1,828
	UTM	12 0319 331E	53 72 446N	NAD27
Dawson Pass		48.48715	-113.47087	7,595/2,315
	UTM	12 0317 427E	53 73 177N	NAD27
A) Begin Off-Trail Route		48.49164	-113.46842	7,964/2,427
	UTM	12 0317 628E	53 73 672N	NAD27
1] Summit		48.49844	-113.46518	9,225/2,811
	UTM	12 0317 888E	53 74 419N	NAD27
2] Lower East Ridge		48.49587	-113.45181	8,035/2,449
	UTM	12 0318 866E	53 74 101N	NAD27

Heading down to Dawson Pass.
n photo: Mike Thompson and Micah Tinkham

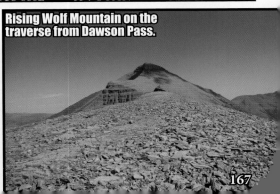

Rising Wolf Mountain on the traverse from Dawson Pass.

Rising Wolf Mountian

SOUTH FACE ROUTE
and
WEST RIDGE ROUTE

Photo taken from helicopter, John VanArendonk photo

TWO ROUTES TO STAND ON THE TWO MEDICINE VALLEY'S HIGHEST PARK

Difficulty: Arduous
GMS Climb Rating: Class III(3) LL
Time Required: 8 -12 hours
Season: July to October
Elevation Change*: 4,384 feet / 1,336 m

* Elevation Change From Trailhead On Featured Route

Elevation: 9,513 feet / 2,899 meters
Rank in Height: 19 of 234
Trailhead: North Shore
U.S.G.S. Topo Map: Mount Rockwell
Trails Illustrated Map: Two Medicine 31
First Recorded Ascent: Unknown

South Face Route
One-way Distance: 4.5 miles / 6.7 km

West Ridge Route
One-way Distance: 10.3 miles / 16.6 km

Date Climbed: _____
Climbed With: _____
Notes:_____
_____
_____
_____
_____
_____

Saintgrizzly" wrote...

"Mahkuyi-opuahsin", the Blackfeet name of this remarkable peak, means *"The way the wolf gets up,"* and on a warm summer day immediately brings to mind wonderful and imaginative visualizations at the unfolding of a lazy wolf as it comes slowly to its feet. This is one of the first (and most immediately dominating) mountains seen when entering the Two Medicine area of Glacier National Park, and that misshapen and lumpy eastern face, as it gives rise to the massive peak behind (the true summit is not visible from the eastern approach) is indeed evocative. I have also seen the mountain on a grim winter day, when its countenance can only be described as emotionally chilling. Rising Wolf is a chameleon, and I most assuredly would not have wished to be confronted by that particular wolf—disturbed, and no doubt cranky—rising through the gloom! The name is memorable, and coming as it does out of an imaginative perception of nature, makes of the mountain something drawing you in. "Rising Wolf."..the words flow gracefully in your mind, a large mountain of real character ... beckoning, calling ...

erhaps it is the vibrant colors oozing out from every square inch of this peak. Perhaps is a royal-blue Two Medicine Lake yielding to lower slopes filled with green vegetation only to be punctuated by patches of snow around the summit. Perhaps it is the enormous cliffs of red and tan that challenge the eye to make out fine details of the space between water and sky. Perhaps it is the two ridges running almost perfectly east and west leading to the summit. Perhaps Rising Wolf Mountain is much more than this! Perhaps?

Rising **Wolf Mountain** is the beast of the Two Medicine Area. It is truly a massive mountain. In other parts of the world it may be referred to as a *massif*, a large mountain mass. It sheer size alone demands attention.

Although its entirety is bounded by hiking trails the most logical place for beginning climbers to climb Rising Wolf is on the *West Ridge Route* from Dawson Pass. An intermediate route, the *South Face Route*, climbs from the north shore of Two Medicine Lake. There are other routes to the summit, such as along the east ridge, that require a high degree of skill and excellent route-finding for experienced climbers.

South Face Route: Depart from the *North Shore Trailhead* (p. 20) and hike approximately 2.4 miles (3.8 km) to a prominent stream bed. The route begins by following the west side of the stream bed.

See the route section for the recommended stream bed. This is different route than the one suggested by Dr. Edwards.

West Ridge Route: Follow the Dawson Pass Trail from the *North Shore Trailhead* (p. 20) to Dawson Pass. The *Sinopah* is also a good option to reduce mileage.

Make sure you do not take the trail to the right at the junction just beyond the bridge. This trail leads to Pitamakan and Cut Bank Passes.

PRACTICE GOOD STEWARDSHIP:

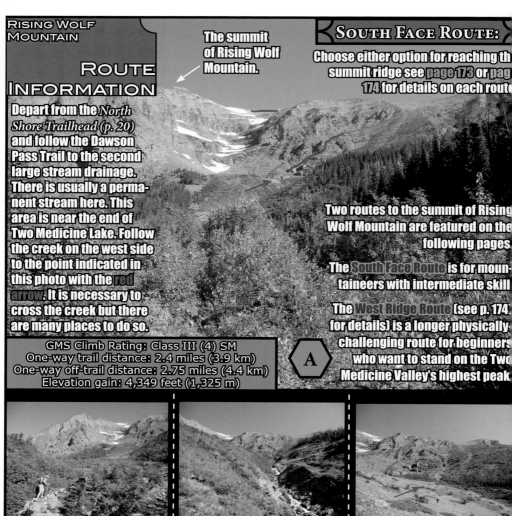

RISING WOLF MOUNTAIN

ROUTE INFORMATION

The summit of Rising Wolf Mountain.

SOUTH FACE ROUTE:

Choose either option for reaching the summit ridge see page 173 or page 174 for details on each route

Depart from the *North Shore Trailhead (p. 20)* and follow the Dawson Pass Trail to the second large stream drainage. There is usually a permanent stream here. This area is near the end of Two Medicine Lake. Follow the creek on the west side to the point indicated in this photo with the red arrow. It is necessary to cross the creek but there are many places to do so.

Two routes to the summit of Rising Wolf Mountain are featured on the following pages

The South Face Route is for mountaineers with intermediate skill

The West Ridge Route (see p. 174 for details) is a longer physically challenging route for beginners who want to stand on the Two Medicine Valley's highest peak

GMS Climb Rating: Class III (4) SM
One-way trail distance: 2.4 miles (3.9 km)
One-way off-trail distance: 2.75 miles (4.4 km)
Elevation gain: 4,349 feet (1,325 m)

A

After reaching the area indicated by the yellow arrows, *both photos indicate same location,* traverse back to the stream bed and climb to the **couloir** then ascend through Class III rock toward the point marked with orange arrow.

Nothing more difficult than Class III will need to be climbed if a safe route is chosen.

1

Help minimize impacts to fragile soil and vegetation.

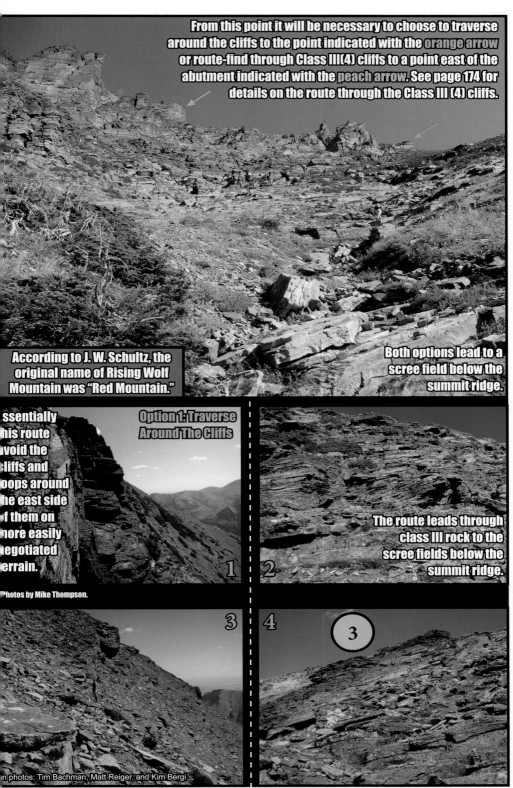

From this point it will be necessary to choose to traverse around the cliffs to the point indicated with the orange arrow or route-find through Class III(4) cliffs to a point east of the abutment indicated with the peach arrow. See page 174 for details on the route through the Class III (4) cliffs.

According to J. W. Schultz, the original name of Rising Wolf Mountain was "Red Mountain."

Both options lead to a scree field below the summit ridge.

Option 1: Traverse Around The Cliffs

ssentially his route void the liffs and oops around he east side f them on more easily egotiated errain.

Photos by Mike Thompson.

1

2

The route leads through class III rock to the scree fields below the summit ridge.

3

4

3

n photos: Tim Bachman, Matt Reiger, and Kim Bergi

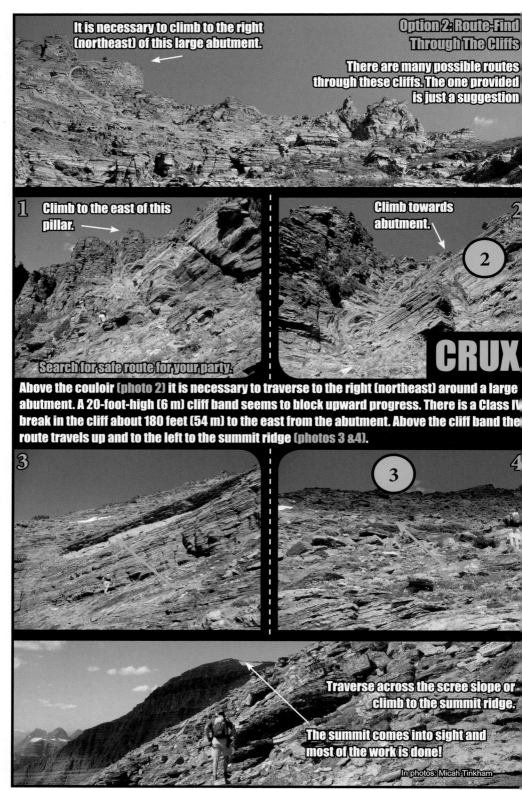

It is necessary to climb to the right (northeast) of this large abutment.

Option 2: Route-Find Through The Cliffs

There are many possible routes through these cliffs. The one provided is just a suggestion

1 Climb to the east of this pillar.

Climb towards abutment. **2**

Search for safe route for your party.

CRUX

Above the couloir (photo 2) it is necessary to traverse to the right (northeast) around a large abutment. A 20-foot-high (6 m) cliff band seems to block upward progress. There is a Class IV break in the cliff about 180 feet (54 m) to the east from the abutment. Above the cliff band the route travels up and to the left to the summit ridge (photos 3 &4).

3

3 **4**

Traverse across the scree slope or climb to the summit ridge.

The summit comes into sight and most of the work is done!

In photos: Micah Tinkham

Do not walk off-trail when the tread is muddy.

Follow the climbers' trail to the point on the summit ridge.

Be extremely cautious if snow blocks the route.

The last "pitch" to the summit.

Make sure you can return to the park. Don't violate Federal Law. See page 17

Looking back on the route.

Scramble through this dark section of rocks by staying on the left (south). This Class III section is quite enjoyable and solid. There are many possibilities for route finding!

4

The last section is a Class II walk-up to the summit cairn.

Get ready for some mind-blowing vistas from the 19th tallest peak in Glacier National Park!

Wear gaiters if mud is deep.

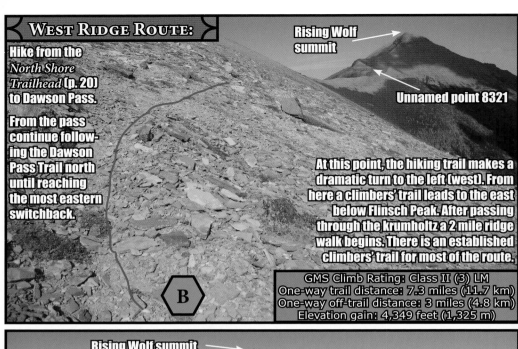

WEST RIDGE ROUTE:

Hike from the *North Shore Trailhead* (p. 20) to Dawson Pass.

From the pass continue following the Dawson Pass Trail north until reaching the most eastern switchback.

Rising Wolf summit

Unnamed point 8321

At this point, the hiking trail makes a dramatic turn to the left (west). From here a climbers' trail leads to the east below Flinsch Peak. After passing through the krumholtz a 2 mile ridge walk begins. There is an established climbers' trail for most of the route.

GMS Climb Rating: Class II (3) LM
One-way trail distance: 7.3 miles (11.7 km)
One-way off-trail distance: 3 miles (4.8 km)
Elevation gain: 4,349 feet (1,325 m)

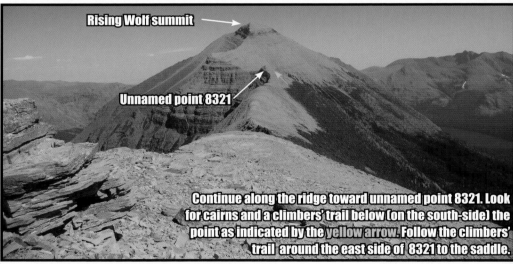

Rising Wolf summit

Unnamed point 8321

Continue along the ridge toward unnamed point 8321. Look for cairns and a climbers' trail below (on the south-side) the point as indicated by the yellow arrow. Follow the climbers' trail around the east side of 8321 to the saddle.

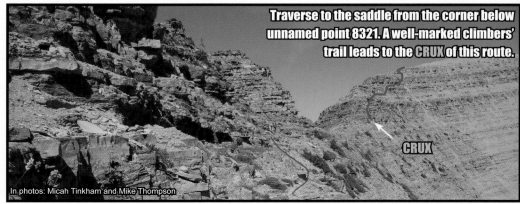

Traverse to the saddle from the corner below unnamed point 8321. A well-marked climbers' trail leads to the CRUX of this route.

CRUX

In photos: Micah Tinkham and Mike Thompson

174

Pick up litter found along the way.

Locate the Class III couloir from the saddle. Continue along the summit ridge above the couloir.

The CRUX as viewed from the saddle.

CRUX

Climb through this Class III couloir. Numerous cairns mark this section of the route.

The dark band of rock blocks progress along the summit ridge. Travel to the right (south) of this band of rocks or scramble through Class III rock on the right edge of the band as indicated with the yellow arrow.

Another slope of loose scree awaits above the dark band. Follow the climbers' trail to the summit.

Photo by Mike Thompson.

Short cutting switchbacks is destructive and illegal.

RISING WOLF
MOUNTAIN

RETURN
ROUTE

CRUX

Once at Dawson Pass follow the Dawson Pass Trail back to the North Shore Trailhead (p. 20) or follow the signs to the upper end boat launch to return on the *Sinopah*.

It is not safe to climb down the South Face Route unless you are ABSOLUTELY sure of the route. A much SAFER descent is to continue west along the ridge towards Flinsch Peak (p.158). Use this photo as a guide to locate the correct route through the two blockages on the ridge.

RISING WOLF
MOUNTAIN

OTHER
OPTIONS

There are few optional climbs other than summiting **Flinsch Peak** (p. 158) via the *East Ridge Route* (p. 164) or **Mount Helen** (p. 150) from Dawson Pass. It may be best to choose one of these options or just call it a great day. Helen has more distance but is less strenuous.

The route to Flinsch Peak is much more solid along the ridge from Rising Wolf than when ascended from Dawson Pass. The top of the couloir is somewhat loose but it is easily avoided. Once on the summit descend down the route down to Dawson Pass rather than descending down the route that was climbed due to being more direct. *See Flinsch Peak for more information.* **A recommended route to the summit of Flinsch Peak from Rising Wolf is outlined in green in the above photo.**

The *Sinopah* cruises to the west end of Two Medicine Lake. Grizzly, Two Medicine Pass, Painted Tepee and Sinopah stand in the distance.
Photo by Mike Thompson

Rockwell, St. Nicholas, Lone Walker, Helen, Phillips

Phillips, Flinsch, Stimson, Morgan, Tinkham, McClintock

Scenic Point, Medicine, Appistoki, Henry, Never Laughs, Bearhead

Select resilient areas such as rocks or snow for rest breaks and other stops.

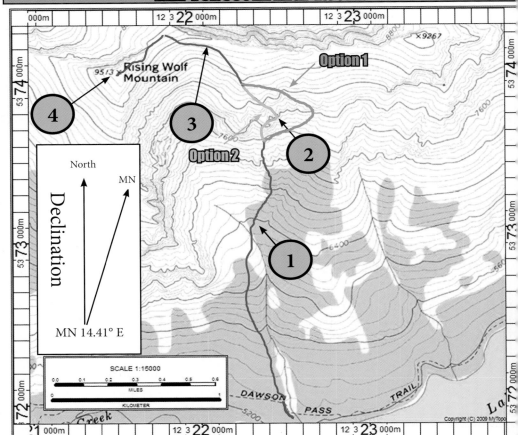

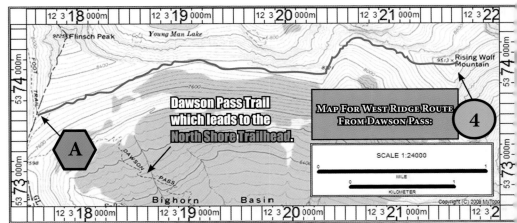

Horses have the right of way.

**Elevations and distances are not exact
due to variations in the chosen route.**

Image provided by mytopo.com

The total off-trail elevation gain for South Face Route to summit is 4,349 feet (1,325 m).
Total off-trail distance is 2.75 miles (4.4 km).

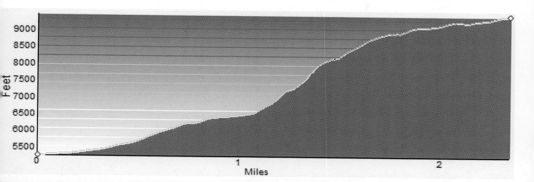

National Geographic Trails Illustrated Maps Glacier/Waterton Lakes National Parks,
Two Medicine (315) shows the approaches to the routes for Rising Wolf Mountain.

**GPS Waypoints are best used in conjunction with
a compass, topo map, and common sense.**

**Relying solely on a GPS for navigation
is NOT recommended.**

	Latitude	Longitude	Elevation (ft/m)
North Shore Trailhead (p. 20)	48.48858	-113.36626	5,129/1,563
UTM	12 0325 162E	53 73 029N	NAD27
A) Begin Off-Trail Route	48.47716	-113.40098	5,238/1,596
UTM	12 0322 556E	53 71 902N	NAD27
1] Point One South Face Route	48.48633	-113.40376	6,182/1,884
UTM	12 0322 382E	53 72 929N	NAD27
2] Point Two South Face Route	48.49380	-113.40195	8,000/2,438
UTM	12 0322 542E	53 73 754N	NAD27
3] Summit Ridge	48.49787	-113.40755	9,200/2,804
UTM	12 0322 143E	53 74 220N	NAD27
4] Summit	48.49614	-113.41505	9,513/2,899
UTM	12 0321 583E	53 74 045N	NAD27
Two Medicine Pass Trail Jct.	48.47786	-113.41842	5,238/1,596
UTM	12 0321 270E	53 72 021N	NAD27
No Name Lake Jct.	48.48113	-113.44484	6,000/1,828
UTM	12 0319 331E	53 72 446N	NAD27
Dawson Pass	48.48715	-113.47087	7,595/2,315
UTM	12 0317 427E	53 73 177N	NAD27
B) Begin Traverse	48.49188	-113.46740	7,960/2,426
UTM	12 0317 700E	53 73 695N	NAD27

Pay attention to the lead rider for instructions.

Mount Morgan

PITAMAKAN OVERLOOK ROUTE

Photo taken from Tinkham Mountain Route.
Photo by Vernon Garner

A SELDOM CLIMBED PEAK WITH UNIQUE VIEWS

Difficulty: Arduous (overall distance)
GMS Climb Rating: Class III (4) LM
Time Required: 8-11 hours
Season: Late June to October
One-way Distance: 9.2 miles / 14.8 km
Elevation Change*: 3,617 feet / 1,102 m

Elevation: 8,781 feet / 2,676 m
Rank in Height: 88 of 234
Trailhead: North Shore
U.S.G.S. Topo Map: Cut Bank Pass, MT
Trails Illustrated Map: Two Medicine 31!
First Recorded Ascent: Unknown

* Elevation Change From Trailhead On Featured Route

Date Climbed: _____
Climbed With: _____
Notes: _____
_____
_____
_____
_____
_____
_____

Mount Morgan sits between Dawson and Cut Bank Passes on the Continental Divide. On a clear day, the views from this area are nothing less than stellar. Mount Stimson, the second tallest peak in the park, dominates the western view and to the north a sea of peaks jut into the skyline. The view to Old Man Lake and Flinsch Peak are outstanding as well!

While Mount Morgan stands in at 8,781 feet (2,676 m) above sea level the off-trail portion of the route is not difficult and takes less than an hour to scramble to the summit cairn.

This peak is most easily climbed while hiking the Dawson-Pitamakan Traverse. There is little information available for the actual route to the summit. Perhaps it is a closely guarded secret by those who have climbed it or perhaps it is such a long distance from the trailheads that those who do make it to the trail below Mount Morgan only have getting back to the trailhead on their mind. Take the extra hour of time and climb this peak. For those in the party that do not wish to summit the trail between the Pitamakan Pass Overlook and Dawson Pass affords excellent views of the climbers on the route.

MOUNT MORGAN

TRAILHEAD INFORMATION

The Pitamakan Pass Trail travels 8.7 miles (14 km) from the **North Shore Trailhead** (p. 20) to the Pitamakan Pass Overlook.

The hike features gorgeous views throughout the trail portion of the

Mount Morgan from the Pitamakan Pass Trail.

trip as it gradually gains elevation from the trailhead. The trail really begins to climb above Old Man Lake but the numerous switchbacks make it quite bearable. There are two junctions at the top of the ridge near Pitamakan Pass. At each junction take the left fork in order to reach the Pitamakan Pass Overlook.

Make sure you are doing plenty of "heybearing" on the trails! This is bear country and bears like the Dry Fork Drainage a lot!

There are no reliable water sources above Old Man Lake so plan accordingly! If you need water fill up at one of the streams from Red Mountain or walk the 0.3 mile (480 m) to Old Man Lake.

Climbers with time to spare can reserve a backcountry campsite at Old Man Lake and make this a two-day trip.

There are also multiple options for extended backpack trips from this location. Secure permits on-line through the park's reservation web-link or get them the day before the trip at one of the Backcountry Ranger Stations.

If you meet riders, step downhill off trail, and stand quietly until they pass.

Scramble up the ridge to the northern corner of Morgan.

A

A large band of limestone blocks progress to the scree fields above the cliffs. There is but one place to safely climb through these cliffs.

Traverse southwest below the limestone wall on scree ledges until locating the chockstone seen in photo below.

The chockstone indicates the entrance to the couloir and the CRUX of the climb.

A fall could be fatal or require crucial medical care that is hours away.

The chockstone is lodged in this wide chimney and is quite prominent.

This location **appears** to be the ONLY SAFE PLACE to climb to the summit without climbing gear.

From this point look to the left and locate the scree-filled couloir, the CRUX that requires a bit of Class III (4) climbing to reach the scree fields below the summit.

Although there appear to be other routes through this 40-50 foot high limestone wall most of them entail great exposure.

If a toilet is not available, carry a trowel and bury feces in a cat-hole, 6-8" deep in

CRUX

The blue bar indicates the same feature in both photographs.

In photos: John VanArendonk

This Class III(4) couloir is the ONLY SAFE WAY to access and return from the summit. Photo by John VanArendonk.

At the top of the CRUX it is necessary to climb up and to the right until reaching the summit ridge.

There are a number of ways to climb to the summit above the CRUX. Find a way that is safe for the skill level for the group.

Remember to mark the location of the top of the CRUX couloir to locate it on the way down.

Heed the warnings regarding attempts to descend elsewhere!

Do not attempt to down-climb other areas of the limestone cliffs. There are unseen overhangs and great exposure and should ONLY be climbed by advanced climbers with gear.

Scramble through scree and cliffs to the summit ridge and follow it to the summit of Mount Morgan!

organic soil, at least 200 ft. from water. Fill and disguise hole and pack out paper.

MOUNT MORGAN

RETURN ROUTE

It does not appear to be safe to down climb **ANYWHERE** else on this peak.

Use the **CRUX** couloir to descend to the trail.

Wall with chockstone.

Cairn marking the top of the couloir.

Top of scree-filled couloir.

Return to the **CRUX** couloir and descend to the scree field below. If the group is continuing to Dawson Pass it is possible to traverse to the south along the scree ledges and then descend to the trail.

If returning to Pitamakan Pass Overlook follow the entire route used to ascend the peak.

MOUNT MORGAN

OTHER OPTIONS

Optional climbs include summiting **Flinch Peak** (p. 158) or **Mount Helen** (p. 150) from near Dawson Pass. It may be best to choose one of these options and then call it a day. Helen has more distance but is less strenuous.

Another option is to scramble to the summit of McClintock Peak which is located directly north of Cut Bank Pass. *This guidebook does not include the route.*

Flinsch Peak and Mount Morgan form the bookends of a saddle which sits over 1,000 feet (304 m) above the Old Man Lake basin.

IT IS NOT ADVISABLE TO DRINK STRONG LIQUORS WHILE CLIMBING IN THE ALPS. IF HOWEVER, YOU ARE GOING TO FALL OVER A CLIFF, IT'S ADVISABLE TO BE THOROUGHLY INTOXICATED WHEN YOU DO SO.

QUOTED FROM AN ENGLISH ALPINIST

We do not advocate drinking alcohol while climbing!

All **Summit View** photos for Mount Morgan were taken during the August 2011 fire season which caused the haze seen in these photos. Climbing on a clear day reveals incredible views!

James, Medicine Grizzly, McClintock, Cut Bank Drainage, Bad Marriage

Flinsch, Rockwell, Helen, Lone Walker, Phillips, Lupfer Glacier

Do your part to preserve the park. Laws preserve the park for everyone to enjoy! See page 17

Urinate on durable surfaces that will not be damaged by animals.

U.S.G.S. Map: Cut Bank Pass
Contour Interval = 80 feet

Image provided by mytopo.com
Map Produced by the U.S. Geological Service

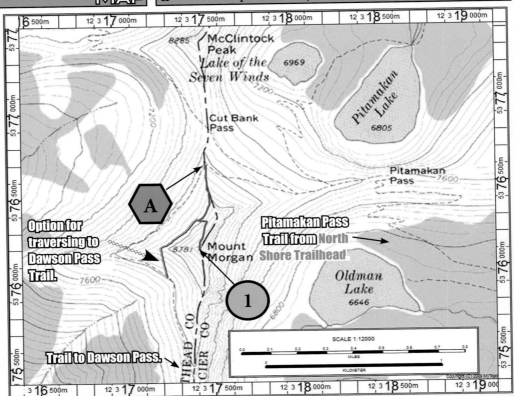

National Geographic Trails Illustrated Maps
Glacier/Waterton Lakes National Parks, Two Medicine (315)
covers the approaches to the routes for Mount Morgan.

Do not down climb anywhere
else on this peak. Follow the
recommended route!

All other ways
are dangerous
without the proper
equipment
and training.

Photo by Matt Fitzwater.

In photo:
John VanArendonk

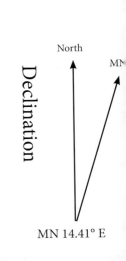

North

MN

Declination

MN 14.41° E

MOUNT MORGAN

ROUTE PROFILE

Elevations and distances are not exact due to variations in the chosen route.

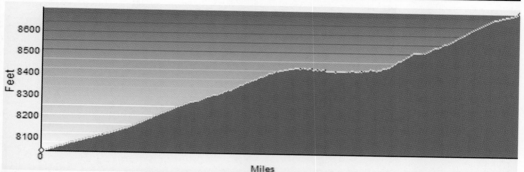

Total off-trail elevation change from the Pitamakan Pass Overlook to summit is 753 feet (229 m) and the total distance is .44 miles (700 m).

MOUNT MORGAN

GPS WAYPOINTS

GPS Waypoints are best used in conjunction with a compass, topo map, and common sense.

Relying solely on a GPS for navigation is NOT recommended.

	Latitude	Longitude	Elevation (ft/m)
North Shore Trailhead (p. 20)	48.48858	-113.36626	5,129/1,563
UTM	12 0325 162E	53 73 029N	NAD27
(A) Pitamakan Pass Overlook	48.51685	-113.47151	9,225/2,811
UTM	12 0317 492E	53 76 680N	NAD27
[1] Summit	48.51403	-113.47195	9,225/2,811
UTM	12 0317 444E	53 76 168N	NAD27

Mount Morgan from the trail to Dawson Pass.

In photo: Blake Passmore and John VanArendonk

Photo by Joey Gardner.

EQUIPMENT:

CRUCIAL TO HAVE:

Day pack
Proper clothing for conditions
Supportive footwear with extra socks
Rain/wind gear (jacket with hood and pants)
Insulating layer (fleece jacket)
Wicking long sleeve base layer
Warm hat and gloves
Water and/or water purification equipment
Food (bring extra just in case)
Sun screen and hat to block sun
Climbing helmet
Bandana (for multiple purposes)
Camera with case
First aid kit
Medication for headaches
Personal medical supplies
Moleskin or duct tape for blisters
Map and compass
Matches/lighter
Flashlight/head lamp
Insect repellent
Counter Assault Bear Deterrent spray

NICE TO HAVE:

GPS
Trekking poles
Scree gaiters
Emergency blanket/bivy sack
Electrolyte mix
Energy gel or power bars
Cell phone
Mini-tripod for group shots
Gloves for scree scrambling

ON AN AS NEEDED BASIS:

Ice axe
Crampons
Camping equipment

QUART BAG SURVIVAL KIT

- Compass
- Multi tool
- Emergency Space Blanket x 2 or 1 blanket and 1 trash bag
- 10-15 ft of small diameter cord/rope
- Small, hotel shampoo bottle filled with fire paste
- Vaseline rubbed cotton balls in a film canister
- Magnesium block & flint or other "spark striker" device
- Old style cigarette lighter with flint and spark wheel
- About 2-3 ft of duck tape wrapped back on itself
- Small LED light preferably with a strobe function
- Extra batteries for electronic navigation devices such as SPOT or GPS
- A few safety pins of varying size
- 1x1 ft piece of aluminum foil
- Signal mirror
- Baggy of Ibuprofen or other stronger pain killer if available

Internet Resources

CLIMB GLACIER NATIONAL PARK:
www.climbglacier.com

CounterAssault:
www.counterassault.com

Glacier Mountaineering Society:
www.glaciermountaineers.com

Glacier National Park Home Page:
www.nps.gov/glac/index.htm

Glacier Shuttle System:
www.nps.gov/glac/planyourvisi

Hammer Nutrition:
www.hammernutrition.com

Bear Safety:

Although there are other brands of bear spray on the market, the authors use and recommend <u>CounterAssault Bear Deterrent Spray</u>. We are thankful that we have never had to use it as well!

The trails and backcountry of Glacier National Park have long been home to grizzly and black bears. Always assume bears are around. Be alert while recreating and use common sense. Carry bear spray at all times while hiking or climbing in the park. It is not unusual to find bears on summits in the late summer and fall. They are up there looking for ladybugs or moths. Bears also frequent the hiking trails.

The best ways to prevent attacks are making noise and staying in groups. Never hike or climb alone. Hike during daylight hours to decrease the odds of a run in with a bear. Call out and make human sounding noises, called "heybearing" in this guidebook, to alert bears of your presence. Stay alert and look for signs of recent bear activities such as digging, bear scat, destroyed logs, and especially carcasses of animals.

Pat Van Emiren photo

In the event of a close contact or attack

Carry bear spray on your hip or chest at all times. **It does no good carrying bear spray in your pack when you need it quickly!** Follow the directions for proper use. If the bear is close get the spray out of its holster. Give the bear plenty of space. Avoid eye contact with the bear; look at its feet or hind legs. Do Not Run! Back out of the area slowly, speak with a soft voice and stay calm. Try to stay upwind so the bear can know what you are.

When a bear first sees you it may stand up on its hind legs making noises with its teeth and swaying its head from side to side. Flattened ears and raised hair may indicate that the bear is aggressive. If it charges with a stiff or bouncy gait it may be a bluff charge.

If the bear charges, pull away the bear spray safety clip. Hold the body of the can in one hand, have the index finger of the other through the trigger hole.

It does no good to fire too soon so wait until the bear is within 20 feet or so. To spray, just pull the trigger. Aim for the bear's face. The spray is colored and you should be able to see it hit the bear. Spray in short bursts rather than one continuous stream. Hopefully the bear with suck the spray into its nasal cavity and turn around and head for the hills. Use this time to continue to retreat down the trail.

Never run. If attacked lie on your stomach or side and draw your legs up to the chest. Clasp your hands over the back of your neck. Grizzly bears generally want to neutralize the threat and once it believes that there is no threat it will generally leave.

For more information on bears and bear attacks see:

www.nps.gov/archive/glac/resources/bears.htm#Hiking

www.counterassault.com

Scott Burry photo

GPS and Mapping Technology:

Global Positioning System (GPS) units can be used to mark waypoints at a location. They give an *approximate* latitude and longitude. Approximate is used here due to a built in variance set by the government to protect national security interests. In this guidebook, in addition to using a GPS, known locations such as trail junctions and summit were located using programs available on-line or as found listed in Glacier National Park reference materials. A GPS unit was used while climbing the routes and then the route was transferred to U.S.G.S. Topo maps from mytopo.com.

Elevation profiles produced with mytopo.com are used with permission.

GPS Waypoints are best used in conjunction with a topo map and common sense. There is a built in variance due to military restrictions and relying solely on a GPS for navigation is **NOT** recommended.

Setting up routes on a GPS:

A route is any group of two or more "Waypoints" that are linked together. When waypoints are linked together it is possible to follow them along a set path that has been entered into a GPS unit. GPS Waypoints are best used with a map, compass and common sense!

Refer to the Owners Manual for your GPS to learn how to set up a route in a GPS Generally the information is found under "Routes" in the Owner's Manual or find it on-line.

Higher quality GPS units produce more accurate data. GPS waypoints are merely a navigation tool that allows the climber to safely follow a route; understand there is a built in variance and the actual point could be 30 to 100 feet away. **Use them as a guide.**

To follow the routes found in this guide book enter each waypoint in order into your GP Route program and follow the route from the trailhead to the summit.

Recommended Maps:

Can you ever have too many maps? In addition to the 1:24,000 scale topo maps there are other maps available for recreating in Glacier National Park.

The standard map, **Glacier National Park**, is produced by the **U.S.G.S.** and the 199 edition adequately covers the park but has no additional features. The scale is 1:100,000

National Geographic Trails Illustrated Maps provide detailed versions in both 1:50,000 scale as well as in 1:100,000 scale (Map # 215). The 1:50,000 scale maps covering Glacier are numbers 313, 314, and 315. This series of maps is an Outdoor Recreatio Map and provides safety tips and a plethora of other information.

Principles Of Leave No Trace:

Please do your part to pass Glacier National Park on to the next generation by using **Leave No Trace** principles. Help keep Glacier National Park clean and pristine!

Plan Ahead and Prepare

Travel and Camp on Durable Surfaces

Leave What You Find

Properly Dispose of Waste

Minimize Campfire Impacts

Respect Wildlife

Be Considerate of Other Visitors

For more information see: www.lnt.org

Peak Comparison Chart:

Having a difficult time deciding which peak to climb? There are so many to choose from and so little time. Use the chart to match fitness, skill level, and time needed to find a suitable climb. See each section for details on the route. BONUS PEAKS are an excellent way to introduce climbers to peak-bagging in Glacier National Park. An * indicates that the peak has a BONUS ROUTE.

Please note: In this chart ELEVATION CHANGE indicates the <u>difference</u> in elevation from the <u>trailhead</u> to the <u>summit</u> of each peak. *See the mountain section for details on elevation gain and loss as they are much greater than the elevation change listed here.*

MOUNTAIN NAME AND PAGE NUMBER	ONE-WAY DISTANCE MILES/KM	ELEVATION CHANGE FEET/M	TIME IN HOURS	GMS CLIMB RATING
FIREBRAND PASS AREA				
Calf Robe Mountain* (34)	6.3 / 10.1	2,840 / 865	4-6	Class II (3) LS
Dancing Lady Mountain (42)	5.5 / 8.8	2,530 / 771	5-7	Class II (3) MS
Red Crow Mountain (50)	5.8 / 9.3	2,783 / 848	5-7	Class II (3) MS
Bearhead Mountain (60)	Varies By Route	Varies By Route	Varies	Class II (3) LL
TWO MEDICINE VALLEY				
Mount Ellsworth* (68)	6.1 / 9.8	3,377 / 1,027	8-10	Class II (3) LM
Mount Henry (78)	5 / 8	3,645 / 1,111	6-10	Class III (4) MM
Appistoki Peak (90)	4.6 / 7.4	2,962 / 902	5-8	Class II (3) MS
Never Laughs Mountain (98)	3.75 / 6	2,510 / 765	5-8	Class III (3) MS
Painted Tepee Peak (106)	8.5 / 13.6	2,519 / 767	6-8	Class III (4) LS
Grizzly Mountain (114)	9.5 / 15.2	3,936 / 1,199	8-12	Class II (4) LM
Mount Rockwell (122)	8 / 12.8	4,141 / 1,262	7-10	Class III (4) LM
Sinopah Mountain (132)	5.2 / 8.37	3,140 / 957	6-8	Class III (4) MM
Lone Walker Mountain (142)	8 / 12.8	3,338 / 1,017	8-10	Class III (4) LM
Mount Helen (150)	7.4 / 11.9	3,406 / 1,038	7-10	Class II (3) LM
Flinsch Peak (158)	Varies By Route	4,096 / 1,248	Varies	Class III (4) LM
Rising Wolf Mountain (168) *South Face Route*	5.15/8.3	4,384 / 1,336	5-7	Class III (4) SM
Rising Wolf Mountain (168) *West Ridge Route*	10.3 / 16.6	4,384 / 1,336	10-12	Class II (3) LM
Mount Morgan (180)	9.2 / 14.8	3,617 / 1,102	8-11	Class III (4) LM
THE BONUS PEAKS				
Scenic Point (88)	3.1 / 5	2,240 / 682	3-6	Class I (1) MS
Bison Mountain (89)				
The Head (89)	7 / 11.3	4,487 /1,367	6-8	Class II (3) MM
Medicine (89)				
Chief Lodgepole Peak (126)	5.4 / 8.6	2,518 / 767	3-6	Class I (1) MS

Glossary Of Terms:

Cairn: A stack of rocks indicating the location of a climbing route (also referred to as ducks).

Chimney: Two opposing rock faces that can be climbed with the right technique.

Chockstone: A rock that is stuck between two opposing walls.

Choss: Loose rotten rock that has a lot of dirt or fine gravel in it. Choss is enjoyable to descend but a drag to ascend. Wearing gaiters helps keep choss and rocks out of boots.

Cleft: A split or crack in an otherwise un-climbable wall that leads to the top of the cliff.

Climb: To move upward, especially by using the hands and feet or the feet.

Climbers' Trail: An unofficial trail that leads climbers to a route.

Consolidated Slope: Scree and soil that forms a compact surface that is easier to walk on while ascending but difficult to walk on while descending.

Couloir: A deep gully on the side of a mountain.

Crux: The most important part of the route, failing to get through the crux may lead to not completing the climb.

Diorite Sill: A 100 foot (30 m) thick formation of light-greenish-gray rock.

Gendarme: Isolated pillars of rock along a ridge.

Goat Trail: A route used by goats, sheep and other critters through Glacier National Park's backcountry that is usually better than any human-made route since they follow the path of least resistance. They have a natural Goat Positioning Sense!

GPS Waypoint: A designated set of coordinates which includes latitude and longitude.

Gully: A narrow, steep-sided channel formed by running water.

Heybearing: Making human noise such as talking, shouting and clapping of hands to alert bears of human presence.

Junction: Where two or more hiking trails or routes meet.

Ledge: An almost horizontal shelf on the side of a mountain that is frequently covered with loose scree or talus.

Lichen: A fungus that grows on rocks. The usual colors are yellow, red and white.

Off-trail: A portion of the route that is not on an official established hiking trail.

On-trail: A portion of the route that travels on the official trail system of the park.

Pillar: An isolated rock formation along a ridge.

Ridge: Where the upper section of two slopes join that lead towards the summit.

Saddle: A low point between two higher ridges or points, also called a pass.

Scramble: To move upward, especially by using the hands and feet or the feet.

Scree: Small loose rock covering a slope.

Spire: A tower-like formation of rock that stands alone.

Summit Cairn: A mound of stones that designates the location of the summit.

Summit, False: A prominent portion of the ridge but not the highest elevation.

Summit, True: The highest elevation on a peak, mount or mountain.

Talus: Larger rock fragments that have accumulated at the base of a cliff or slope.

Trailhead: Where a hiking trail begins and ends, see pages 20-21.

Traverse: To go up, down, or across (a slope) diagonally.

For Updates Like Us On FaceBook

WWW.FACEBOOK.COM/CLIMBGLACIERNATIONALPARK

On Picasa follow
Climb Glacier National Park
to see more photos!